Millican Dal

A Search for Romanc

Copyright © M.D. Entwistle 2004

First Edition published 2004 by

Mountainmere Research

69 Harwood Road, Rishton, Blackburn, Lancashire. BB1 4DH

info@mountainmere.co.uk

British Library Cataloguing in Publication Data

A catalogue record for this book is available from the British Library

ISBN

0-9547213-0-6

Updates and multimedia available from

www.professor-of-adventure.com

Millican Dalton

A Search for Romance & Freedom

This book is dedicated to all aspiring 'Daltonites'.

Contents.

1	Preface.	1
2	The First Years.	3
3	Vocational Rethink.	11
4	Camping Holidays.	14
5	Professor of Adventure.	20
6	Robin Hood or Robinson Crusoe?	25
7	Dietary Values.	30
8	You're My Rock.	34
9	The Fell and Rock Climbing Club.	41
10	The Epping Camp.	47
11	My First Leader.	50
12	Safe and Sound.	60
13	The Tirol.	65
14	High Heavens Camp.	74
15	The 'Cave Hotel.'	78
16	Rogue Herries and Millican Dalton.	85
17	Elementary my dear Watson.	88
18	The Caveman 1941.	90
19	Farewell Millican Dalton.	97
20	Epilogue.	101
21	Acknowledgements.	104
22	Index.	105

Millican Dalton
Professor of Adventure

1
Preface.

"Why?" was the question I asked upon first hearing of a character that quit employment to live life as he pleased. Millican Dalton's choice to become a mountaineering guide and live in tents, caves and huts and his extraordinary life in general seemed to be quite incomprehensible. Why would someone make such a decision? Why did he dislike conventional living? Why did he have to live in the outdoors?

It would be safe to assume that the majority of the working population would like to follow in Dalton's footsteps and finish work for good to pursue their own dreams. I am one of those people and his tale was something of an inspiration.

My purpose in writing this book is the result of a search for answers and a desire to learn more. After a preliminary inspection of this character it became apparent that very little was actually known. I harvested only limited and vague information from books and magazines with much of it containing anomalies, contradicting statements and deviations from the truth. I was therefore in more or less the same position as when I started – none the better for my discoveries. If I was to find out more the only way forward was to research the man myself. Having ample spare time, knowledge of researching and a serious determination to unearth the truth, I proceeded to collate information through a systematic approach. The material in this book comes from a wide variety of sources. Many institutions had to be visited around the country such as county record archives, libraries and the like. Valuable and indispensable anecdotes were obtained through interviews with those who knew him in one capacity or another and from scores of letters, emails and telephone conversations.

An undertaking of this nature was not an easy task and many stumbling blocks were encountered en-route. Sources of information proved difficult to locate, many existed but tracing them was a different matter. Some people are more than forthcoming with information; others are definitely not. The spelling of his name, which should be simple, was most problematic, with such mistakes ranging from Millicent, Milligan, Milean to the most lackadaisical William, leading to identification difficulties. However, such complications formed part of the investigation. As information became fruitful, a fascinating story began to unfold which was completely encapsulating. I knew I was on the trail of a great story and the completion of the project was simply a matter of course.

Whilst this book is a biography it is not intended to be a distinguished piece of literature or a complete history. To write a comprehensive biography on such a subject would be nigh on impossible. Some of the better known biographical subjects leave memoirs, diaries, letters and other personal effects which simplify the research process enabling a quicker, more detailed picture to be built. This was not the case with Dalton – no memoirs, no diaries. However, by researching as widely as possible I hope to have portrayed an accurate and interesting picture. It was my intention to give the reader an insight into the life of an incredible human being, his way of thinking and his daily experiences. This book forms a link between past and present and serves as a reminder to all who are engrossed in busy modern day life the importance of simple living and the real reasons for life – not the pursuance of material items, but of genuine happiness. I believed it was essential to preserve such an inspirational true-life story for future generations, as with the passing of time, people and the destruction of written information, the facts can be lost for ever.

Consequently this is the story of Millican Dalton – Professor of Adventure.

M. D. Entwistle BSc (Hons)
December 2002

2
The First Years.

"Forty years ago I was working as a clerk in a city office. Day after day I went to the office at the same time. But this was not the life for me. I gave up my job in the commercial world and set out to seek romance and freedom," he told the Sunday Chronicle correspondent in 1933 whilst clinging to a large beech tree. Sacrificing a life of comfort and ease at the age of 36 was Millican Dalton's boldest decision and saw him embark on a lifelong quest for thrills and adventure. He was to receive nationwide publicity as the Professor of Adventure and would prove to live a lifestyle that was in stark contrast from his upbringing in Nenthead.

Nenthead village, England's highest, was originally in a remote area of southeast Cumberland surrounded by the rugged Pennine landscape, situated adjacent to the borders of Durham and Northumberland. The discovery of vast quantities of lead and zinc, which could be viably mined, resulted in the London Lead Company, also known as The Quaker Co., purchasing much of the land around Nenthead. They subsequently expanded an original smelt mill and mine, making it one of the first purpose built industrial villages in Britain.

The London Lead Company played a major role in the development of the village and the surrounding area, providing high standards of education and social welfare. Nenthead

Foulard – Millican Dalton's birthplace.

was basically born through the necessity of homes for mine employees, jobs were plentiful and the population boomed. Practically all those who lived in or around Nenthead worked for the London Lead Company.

William Dalton, a Quaker, was one such employee who worked as a smelt mill agent and lived on the outskirts of the village at Foulard with his wife Frances. She was part of the Millican family from Alston and stayed at home to raise their seven children – five boys and two girls. As was the norm the wife's maiden name was used as a child's forename and so, unsurprisingly, the second youngest child was named Millican Dalton.

Millican Dalton was born on the 20th April 1867 in the family home at Foulard. He was actually the second child to bear the name but the first, Lucy Millican Dalton, died at the age of two and half in 1860. The eldest brothers, William Tinniswood Dalton (b.1854), John James Dalton (b.1856) and Joseph Crosby Dalton (b.1858) had reached their teens by the time Millican was born and already living away from home at boarding school. Elizabeth Crosby Dalton (b.1865) and Henry George Dalton (b.1868) completed the family.

Further bad fortune struck again when Millican was only seven. In 1874 William Dalton died of heart disease on The Grove in Ilkley, Yorkshire, at the age of 47 where he had been seriously ill for two weeks. His body returned home and was interred in Alston Cemetery. Frances, now widowed with three siblings to raise, fortunately had the help of family and friends. An annuity paid to widows of L.L.C. employees eased financial worries and additional help was received from her father, Tinniswood Millican. Evidently he was a wealthy and influential man, highly esteemed and well known for his business capabilities. He was also superintendent of the L.L.C. and responsible for lead mining operations in Weardale (Stanhope and Ronaldkirk), in Dufton and in Alston Moor.

To ensure the success of their strict non-denomination education system the L.L.C. required all children to receive schooling from the age of six. Accordingly all the Dalton children attended Nenthead School until the age of 11 or 12 and then boarded at Brookfield School, also known as Friend's School, Wigton, Cumberland. Pupils were nominated by a Quaker overseer and paid £16 each per annum. School records, currently held at Carlisle Records Office, indicate that none of the children were Quakers or even members of the Allendale Quaker Monthly Meeting. However, William Dalton was a Quaker and on these grounds admission was preliminary granted. According to reports forwarded to Brookfield School, Millican had made "very good progress in reading, writing and arithmetic" and based on this he was accepted as a pupil on 15th January 1878.

The Brookfield education was intensive and the teachings rather more advanced than in Nenthead. Subjects studied as part of the curriculum ranged from ornithology, entomology, meteorology, gardening, astronomy, chemistry and human physiology to French and Latin. Each day was lived in strict accordance with the school rules and was twelve hours long. Commencing at 7am, pupils rose an hour earlier and were expected to be

Brookfield schoolwork 1880.

prepared for a day in fear of the Lord.

Millican soon showed an interest in the activities of the school and became a member of the Band of Hope on the 24th April 1878. This was a temperance organisation for working class children, who along with their teachers had a common goal to remain habitual abstainers from intoxicating liquors. Membership was through written application with a signed pledge: "I agree to abstain from intoxicating liquors as beverages." Efforts by all members helped educate public opinion so that the evils of the demon drink could be diminished and finally abolished. Music played an important role with competitions held between different Band of Hope choirs. Meetings conducted once a term comprised of lectures and teachings concerning the problems associated with alcohol. As a reward, days out such as visits to the seaside were arranged on a regular basis. Furthermore to his membership of the Band of Hope was his election as curator of the Cabinet Class (a collection of curiosities ranging from an Oriole's nest to roman pottery). It was his responsibility to maintain and catalogue the growing collection of artefacts donated by various members of the community.

From around the mid-1870's the lead industry had fallen into decline due to cheap imports and over the next decade levels of unemployment rose. Population figures for Nenthead plunged by a fifth after scores of families emigrated to the Americas and Australia in search of work.

With these problems in mind, Frances considered a move south to north London. Several years prior in the summer of 1873 Millican's aunt, uncle and cousins had already made the move settling at 92 Bishopsgate Street, Middlesex, to manage a carpet warehouse. A decision was made for her when Tinniswood Millican died at home in West

Nenthead House on April 2nd, 1879. Since William had also died and unemployment was rising there was nothing to keep the family in the region. The children, all well educated, would be limited for employment at their level. With extended family already living in the city, it therefore seemed a logical destination.

Soon after Tinniswood Millican's death, Frances, Joseph and Elizabeth, along with aunt Isabella F. Burns, James L. Burns and 14-year-old servant girl Annie Thomson from Nenthead, moved into number 3 Brownswood Road, Middlesex. Funding a move to the capital was not too much of a problem. Frances still received an annuity from the L.L.C., which, with income from her ample inheritance and board and lodgings from the others, was sufficient for her needs. Although the family had moved, Millican and Henry remained at Brookfield school where they studied until 22nd December 1880, before leaving to live in London fulltime. It is uncertain whether the two brothers continued with their education.

3 Brownswood Road, London.

Frances had made a wise decision to move. The need to migrate south for a better future had been justified but nevertheless proved to be a huge culture shock to all concerned. For years they had benefited from copious amounts of fresh air, big skies and rolling countryside but suddenly found themselves in a new world of hustle and bustle and the misery of the dreaded London Smog. Over the years smog related deaths rose remorselessly with the worst tragedy experienced in 1880 when 2,000 people died in one week. It was a major scourge of Victorian London and left many with respiratory diseases.

Not totally happy with their new surroundings the Daltons soon decided to move again and in a bid to find a cleaner, more attractive area to live, chose a home in Highams Park, Chingford, Essex. It was at the junction of Castle Avenue and The Avenue and was larger than Brownswood Road, had the added benefit of a garden and was reasonably distant from the city. The Victorian house was of architectural character and featured a turret on one corner. This is where Millican had his room.

By now the boys had become more daring and increasingly adventurous, having grown out of their usual playtime habits. Upon acquiring a length of genuine Alpine rope, Millican began looking for ways in which it could be used. Eventually he found that the usual descent from his room to the garden was rather too conventional so he constructed a rope ladder, secured it out of the window and used it in preference to the stairs. As a treat for his brothers, Millican would sometimes let Joseph and Henry make the defiant journey downwards.

Neighbours also found themselves drawn into the vertical manoeuvres emanating from his bedroom window. Willing boys, hauled from the ground to the dizzying heights of the turret in Alpine fashion, were directed to paddle with their arms in order to avoid colliding with the glazed kitchen roof and to continue until they reached the sanctuary of the attic window two stories above the ground. His 'tuition' was also passed onto friends Jack and Mary and neighbours Dorothy and brother. Although their average age was only seven they quickly learnt to climb trees. On one occasion pseudo 'Uncle Millican' had them astride the branch of an old elm tree when their horrified mothers returned shrieking "Like so many birds on a bough?"

In future years Millican became particularly enthusiastic about tree climbing or "boling." This involved traversing and ascending large oak or beech trees – or any tree with a coarse bark. Substantial trunks offered cracks, chimneys, cols and face climbs and provided excellent substitutes to rock faces.

The brothers' spirit of adventure, although in its early stages, then progressed onto recreational camping, which had recently been invented. After obtaining a tent, the intrepid brothers ventured on weekend camping expeditions to nearby Epping Forest. Hour upon hour was spent in the forest improving their camping, campcraft and tree climbing skills.

It was on one such expedition that Henry challenged Millican to a fire lighting contest. It was a damp and cold winters day in the thick of the Forest. Snow on the ground increased the difficulty of the task, as the wood was wet. Nevertheless, Millican took up the offer and agreed that no artificial means other than matches should be used. As a wind up, Henry secretly produced some firelighters from inside his coat, which enabled his fire to instantly catch hold. Millican, who was initially amazed, soon discovered the fraudulent act and was not too pleased. On another occasion when offered a thin slice of soap masquerading as cheese between two crackers his remarks were unrepeatable. It was clear at this stage that he was not particularly noted for his sense of humour.

After years of fun and adventure it was time to face up to reality. Millican faced the prospect of employment and, like Joseph, entered the mundane world of insurance. It was in the heart of the City of London, at 81 Cornhill, that he worked as a Fire Insurance Clerk for the Union Assurance Society (Fire and Life). Good wages allowed for a better than average way of life with sufficient money available to fund the much enjoyed camping expeditions which had become a major element of his life. Incidentally Henry also entered the insurance sector.

Upon reaching his late teens Millican, accompanied by brothers and friends, roamed further afield to the Lake District, Scotland and Wales to camp. It was a natural progression with more options available and the chances of adventure increased, indeed these areas, amongst others, were the places to be for the Victorian tourist. Rather than carry equipment in rucksacks, which would have not been possible, they loaded vast weights of blankets and heavy canvas tents onto their bicycles. Use of a bicycle for the transportation of equipment was the equivalent of a porter's trolley. This proved awkward though, as the excessive amounts of gear prevented the bicycles from being ridden and consequently they had to be pushed to their destination. On nearing their proposed camp, more often than not in fading daylight, a last push would be made up tracks like Sty Head Pass, an activity at that time known as "pass storming." They would finally pitch their tents in total darkness, most of the time not knowing their exact position. Understandably, jaunts of this nature took much planning, packing and proved to be rather hard work.

For years the Dalton brothers struggled with large amounts of heavy equipment but during the 1880's Millican and Henry began tinkering with gear in a bid to make transportation and handling in general more bearable. Their pioneering developments made real progression upon learning of Thomas Hiram Holding's research into lightweight camping. His vast knowledge of camping skills derived from a 1200 mile crossing of the American prairies in 1853. In 1877 he then made a journey to the Highlands of Scotland where he camped and cruised the Lochs in a canoe, which was the first method of transport for the early recreational camper. He was in fact the founder of modern recreational camping. Prior to recreational camping, tents had been reserved for the likes of gypsies, the military and vagabonds. Holding, a tailor, gathered with friends in the rear of his shop on Maddox Street, London, where they discussed ideas on reducing weight. Eventually after much analysis of individual items of kit, an outfit weighing in at only ten pounds was developed which could be carried in the poaching pocket of a Norfolk jacket. Considering the limitations of available materials, this was an amazing feat.

The design and manufacture of lightweight equipment was all well and good but it still needed transporting. If the canoe was the first recreational camping vehicle, the bicycle was definitely the second. Lightweight cycle camping roused a great deal of interest within the outdoor fraternity, providing the ability to carry smaller loads more quickly and easily over greater distances. Dalton, an early cycle camper, also used his own lightweight gear in preference to heavy packs. Lightweight tents, cooking utensils, food and clothing could be loaded onto his bike and, although generally ridden, still had to be pushed to its destination on many occasions, but nevertheless proved much easier to control.

Holding, also a cycle camping enthusiast wrote a book on the subject titled *Cycle and Camp* (Warde Locke 1898). Twelve readers of this book, who remain unknown, showed their interest and immediately contacted Holding. Three years later in 1901 he formed the Association of Cycle Campers, thought to be the first camping club in the world and now known as the Camping and Caravanning Club. The first meet, in the foundation year, comprised of just six members, including Holding. These stalwarts cycled from London, Bath and Birmingham with their specially devised lightweight kit and camped in Ickleton Road on the outskirts of Wantage, Oxfordshire. As a participating cycle camper, Dalton soon became a member and joined at some point between the Club formation and 1907.

An early portrait c. 1900.
(Mayson Collection)

A relationship with Holding is unclear, but they undoubtedly knew each other on a personal basis. It is generally assumed in some circles that Millican Dalton helped in the creation of the Club. Supporting this claim was the Essex Review 1948 which clearly stated his involvement. However, material held in the archives of the Camping and Caravanning Club shows no such participation, although as these archives remain incomplete his part played in the Club's orchestration cannot be categorically ruled out. Also contrary to belief, again according to archived material, he was never Club President and very unlikely to have been a District President.

With the dawn of the "Golden Era" of British rock climbing, the sport received much publicity after Walter Parry Haskett-Smith had soloed Napes Needle in 1886. Learning of this and of other great climbing feats, the Dalton brothers, ever keen for new experiences, set out some time around the late 1880's in the footsteps of great names such as J. W. Robinson, Slingsby and Haskett-Smith. Years of tree climbing had set the scene for rock climbing to which they soon became empowered, finding the associated exercise, scenery and exposure exhilarating.

Already familiar with the Lake District, in particular the Borrowdale valley, the brothers searched for their own piece of rock and began to combine cycle camping with rock climbing, the all important climbing gear was easily carried on their bikes. With free time restricted by work patterns and the inconvenience of travel from the south, public holidays provided the only sufficient time for extended camping jaunts. Scafell was considered the ideal mountain to camp under, with Wasdale the choice for many Christmas, Whitsuntide and Easter trips. Wasdale provided close proximity to the large crags and high fells and was the birthplace of British rock climbing.

It appears that over time Millican became engrossed in the outdoor scene and felt that work was beginning to interfere with leisure. An urge for a life in the open developed. Realising that his leisure pursuits gave him the ability for appropriate self-expression and a feeling of complete happiness, he contemplated the idea of becoming a mountaineering guide.

3
Vocational Rethink.

'Millican Dalton Easter 1913'. (Dale Collection)

Millican felt far from happy in the commercial world of fire insurance and had not been employed long before he realised it was dull, repetitive and boring. "I felt stifled," he said "Day after day I went to the office at the same time. But this was not the life for me." He felt an overwhelming sense of constriction, like a caged wild animal. He wanted to be free and live a more adventurous and varied life. In fact he was willing to treat his life as a chemical experiment.

Initially, in order to overcome his unhappiness, he decided to escape the chaos of the City, at least to some degree, by acquiring a plot of land in the rural farming community of Thornwood, North Weald, Essex. Dalton's plot, referred to as "Esperenca," was a permanent base on which home was made amongst extensive hectares of farmland in nothing more than a tent sometime between 1893 and 1901. However, the 20-mile commute into the City and the continual boredom of day-to-day working life still proved too much.

Consequently, a philosophy was developed in which he firmly believed – a philosophy that enabled him to live and not just exist. The foundation of his theory of life, as far as can be ascertained, was concerned with romance, freedom and escapism, focusing on issues such as simplicity, pacifism and truth and was intended to prevent a return of that stifling sensation. Lifestyle, pastimes and ideals worked in perfect harmony, all forming part of a determination to shape a better future and to create a new life. Without any hint of selfishness or self-importance, the harmony of his philosophy revolved around himself and himself only. A non-conformation with societies expectations was number one priority.

Armed with this newfound, life changing philosophy and motivated and guided by desire he pursued his goal of freedom wholeheartedly. Realising that a self-sufficient existence was achievable funded by means of a small, private income, it was without hesitation that Dalton exchanged convention for self-fulfilment in 1904. "I gave up my job in the commercial world and set out to seek romance and freedom," said Dalton proudly.

Characteristics of romance, the imaginative projection of the real world, include an examination of personality and the potential of the mind, a focus on one's passions and creative spirit at the cost of rules and protocol; and a greater appreciation of the beauties of nature. Through adopting these notions and looking at life in a different perspective – basically through rose coloured spectacles – life in general could be carefree and more fun, even downbeat situations could be perceived as idealistic.

So he resigned from his job at the Union Assurance Society but decided to remain on his plot of land. He soon became accustomed to his newfound freedom and was basically thankful for the opportunity to live in the outdoors as a way of life.

Clarifying the benefits of camping in a future *Fell and Rock Climbing Club Journal* (1913, titled *A Camping Holiday*) he wrote:

"Camping provides the completest possible change from ordinary civilised town existence; and, being the healthiest kind of life, as well as the jolliest and most unconventional, is the best antidote to the rush and stress of city work. The open-air life has been found by experience to be a *cure*, not a cause, of rheumatism, as it is likewise for consumption and neurasthenia. Among the many advantages camping has over house or hotel, the chief is that one is in the open air in view of the ever-varying aspects of mountain, lake and river, from getting up to bedtime. Camping also combines perfectly with other open-air sports and pursuits – such as rowing, mountaineering, fishing, swimming, painting, botanising, and the study of wildlife."

This article is of significant interest and provides a firsthand insight into what factor health may have possibly played in his decision to quit work. Without doubt he considered the outdoor life to be a *cure* and not a *reason* for rheumatism, consumption and neurasthenia. Did he *experience* the *cures* himself, or was it a family member or friend? Considering that, when the article was written, Dalton had lived outdoors for around 20 years, it would appear that he was in fact referring to his own vast wealth of experience. It is possible then, with the impression that he gives, a degree of ill health, perhaps acquired whilst living in the thick of the London smog, contributed to his alternative lifestyle.

Did he really suffer from rheumatism and did the exercise of "open-air sports" ease the pain? Was Millican Dalton seeking the "open-air life" as a treatment for consumption, better known as tuberculosis? Consumption plagued thousands of Londoners for which Victorian doctors commonly prescribed fresh air. To what extent, if any, did he suffer neurosis? Was his self-help approach and his "antidote to the rush and stress of city work" intended to cure the problem? Symptoms, amongst others, include mild depression and a difficulty in relating to the immediate environment, but without loss of reality and repression. As repression prevents adequate self-expression it would also provide an explanation to why he wanted to search for freedom.

Whatever the truth behind these health issues his direction in life had taken a drastic turn. Not only was his camp noticeably fresher than previous southern residences, it also provided an antidote to the symptoms of conventional modern day living. Other residents, mainly of a similar genre, made up the small community. Immediately adjacent was shipping clerk, Ernest Pollard, who had also chosen a life under canvas. The Flemings, Neales and Foresters made bricks and mortar homes their preference.

Soon after the dawn of the 20th Century and after several contented years in Thornwood a move was made, for whatever reason, eastward to Billericay, Essex. At this stage Billericay was totally rural and, as many could not afford housing anyway, simply made their homes from shacks, tents and the like. Indeed it was a great plot land area, much of it owned by the wealthy Petre family. On his acre of land, aptly named "The Camp," was the careful cultivation of a fruit and vegetable garden.

Family and friends, given no say in the matter, quickly learnt to accept and appreciate his simple living, high thinking, down-to-earth and straightforward philosophy of life, although many thought he was somewhat unconventional. With work a distant memory, sufficient time was available to concentrate on the important issues in life such as self-expression, holidays, outdoor pursuits and the establishment of his guiding business.

4
Camping Holidays.

A Professor of Adventure postcard c.1920's.
(Mayson Collection)

Millican's ambitions had altered vastly from his hopes of ten years before whilst still a scholar. Long gone was any ambition to be successful in the commercial world – that was left to other members of his family. Instead his dream of working as a mountaineering guide started to become reality. Word of his new profession quickly spread and within no time he was guiding groups to Switzerland, Austria, Ireland, Wales, Scotland and the English Lake District.

Offering a wide range of activities distinguished Dalton from other guides of the day who simply promoted guiding for walking and climbing. His multi-activity holidays, surely some of the first, included the usual walking and climbing, but also integrated expert tuition in camping and outdoor cuisine, ghyll scrambling, rapid shooting, rafting, canoeing and sailing – basically the complete experience.

Advertisement of his services was more than just through word of mouth. Posters placed around Keswick in shop windows such as Maysons' and Abrahams' photographic studios and in Arden's bookshop promoted "Camping Holidays, Mountain Rapid Shooting, Rafting, Hairbreadth Escapes." Elsewhere placards publicised "Camping and Tramping in the English Lakes." A close friend and climbing partner, Ralph H. Mayson, whose family owned a photographic business on Lake Road, produced a series of picture postcards, which Dalton signed and gave to clients. Some prints included his address and doubled as business cards. It was an ideal partnership; Mayson loved to take photographs and Dalton enjoyed striking a pose and made a magnificent subject, becoming the centrepiece of his artistry on many occasions. Besides advertising his services, the Lake Road emporium also sold the series of postcards. These postcards, more than affordable, had become a favourite holiday souvenir. Mayson, who rarely left Lakeland, referred to him as "a true gentleman of the hills," which was probably the reason he became something of a favourite amongst the ladies.

Meanwhile, Henry George Dalton was taking his own photographs. He was an amateur photography enthusiast who had something of an eye for a good picture. Late Victorian and Edwardian photography in the Lakes was dominated by the commercial work of the Abrahams and Maysons, but in all fairness, Henry's photographic work is just as historically important. The Abrahams and Maysons concentrated on landscapes and climbing shots, whilst Henry specialised in camping with campfire scenes a specific favourite.

The lighting of fires, production of outdoor fare and pitching of tents was a fundamental part of all holidays and received comprehensive explanation. Whilst an important and fun element of outdoor life the excitement of these skills was increased in remote locations, Dalton made the point "I would like to tell of many wild expeditions – in Scotland, a three days 'trek' across Rannoch Moor, bivouacking in the open without a tent, passing thro' the dark defile of the Pass of Glencoe at midnight. "Over the sea to Skye," we pitched our tent in the savage solitude of Loch Coruisk, walled in by the Cullin Hills, whose rugged ridges provide the finest rock climbing in Britain; of Kenmare Estuary and Killarney; of Christmas and Easter camps by Scafell; and of camps in Switzerland at the foot of the mighty Matterhorn."

Scotland, Wales and the English Lake District, Britain's equivalent to the Swiss Alps, offered similar spectacular scenery and fresh air and therefore became popular destinations. It was in the Lakes that Dalton taught the majority of his clients the skills and safety aspects of rock climbing, introducing many first timers to the most thrilling of sports. Novice climbers, generally taken on easier routes, enjoyed jaunts to Pillar Rock – New West, North Climb, Walkers Gully, Central Jordan and Pendlebury Traverse; to Napes Needle on Great Gable and Doves' Nest in Combe Ghyll.

Unfortunately, rock climbing was subject to climatic change, but never one to be deterred by bad weather, the excitement continued whatever the sky could unleash with his clients shown the unexpected benefits of heavy rain. The northern lakes, harbouring England's wettest spots, provided ideal wet weather conditions for ghyll scrambling in Lodore Falls or Stanley Ghyll in Eskdale whilst in spate.

Indeed by many he became known as the "Skipper" for his high regard for water sport, he was as well renowned for sailing as he was for climbing. Surprisingly the pleasure of sailing and rowing was not restricted to daylight hours. Reminiscing, Dalton continued "At midnight there was still a lingering afterglow when the full moon rose above the Fells of Borrowdale, behind the three little white tents. A girl in the party proposed a row, so four of us commandeered a boat, and rowed the two miles down the winding Derwent, and onto the open lake. Broken silver edged clouds drifted across the moon, and as we pulled lazily along, misty, wispy vapours rose from the surface of the water, veiling and unveiling the surrounding wall of mountains. Landing on one of the wooded islands, we made a big blazing fire of sticks, boiled water in an oatcake tin, put in some slabs of chocolate which one man happened to have in his pocket, dug out some old Swiss-milk tins for drinking vessels, and with some oatcake, had a light impromptu "supper of the Savage Club," and talked of past adventures. Re-embarking, the star-spangled sky was perfectly clear, with faint indications of the approaching dawn. It was four o'clock when we got back to camp, quite ready for the sleep deferred."

'Rafting on Derwentwater'. (F.& R.C.C. Collection)

The genteel pastime of rowing could be replaced by the buzz of mountain rapid shooting if faster action was required. This was more often than not undertaken on the three mile northerly course of the River Derwent which connects Derwentwater with its twin lake, Bassenthwaite, because according to Dalton "Shooting the numerous rapids in its course, and getting the boat back again upstream, provides as exciting and novel a sport as to be had anywhere in the British Isles." Interestingly and indicating the exclusivity of his holidays he added, "Our camp crews are the only passengers up that river."

If his crews acted as the only passengers on the river, then they were probably the only people rafting on the lake. In the summer of 1912 Dalton and several of his party played potted "Peter Pan" on Derwentwater. Explaining the construction of the raft Dalton wrote, "I discovered some felled trees lying in a wood on the shore; some of them were 35 feet long, and took five men to shift into the water. We lashed seven of these trunks

16

securely together with an Alpine rope, and found the raft would carry a crew of five. We used branches as paddles, and went a long way out from the shore. I also rigged up a Scotch plaid as a sail."

It seems whatever the shape or style of raft; the recipe for fun was only two steps away, the addition of Millican Dalton and water. Whatever the activity, nature's delights, specifically botany and geology, would be pointed out en-route.

Hairbreadth escapes occurred on practically every expedition – or did as far as clients were concerned! An account of such an expedition was detailed by R. K. Vinycomb and published in the first newsletter of the Northumberland Mountaineering Club dated December 1948. This described an adventure to a gully on Scafell during rough weather at an Easter weekend camp in Wasdale around 1912. After stopping to eat lunch the large party gathered at the start of Deep Ghyll and roped themselves together. Upon the discovery of a peregrines' nest and supposedly due to the curious "peregrinations" they jestingly christened the route "Peregrines Gully." Rather than carry their rucksacks they decided to leave them in the little cave that remained unblocked by 25 feet of snow. After passing over a lengthy snow slope the party was challenged with a substantial ice bulge. This was at the top of the next pitch

Rafting opposite the Lodore Hotel, Derwentwater.

and was overcome by cutting steps. With half the party having safely negotiated the icy obstacle, weather conditions took a turn for the worse and a serious blizzard advanced. With no pause in the blizzard it took the group until midnight to reach camp and George's farm lodgings where they devoured a well-deserved meal of ham and eggs. The "Skipper" had decided to lead his party off by the West Wall Traverse. To make the situation worse the route was blanketed with thick, mirrored ice and gave all cause for concern, with most happy to have survived, yet experienced, an hairbreadth escape.

Importantly, all guiding was carried out with the addition of his philosophy that was well and truly being lived out. Dalton experimented with new attitudes and introduced mixed-sex groups. These groundbreaking activities were seen as highly controversial by guardians of traditional values and common decency who believed such activities would encourage loose behaviour. However, commonsense prevailed and the mixed-sex group trips continued. "The charms of camping are well known and keenly appreciated by a growing number of holidaymakers of both sexes," wrote Dalton.

To augment his income, especially during the winter months, Millican, as a seasoned camper, began producing camping equipment that was sold by recommendation. Innovative equipment, designed around his experiences, was purposely of a lightweight concept long before it was freely available. At first, manufacture was by hand, but the acquisition of a sewing machine made the process faster and soon he was producing many lightweight cotton tents, unframed rucksacks and sleeping bags.

Designs varied from wall tents, bell tents and tepees to bivouacs. In order to ensure the tents remained lightweight, yet waterproof and durable, their manufacture benefited from a fine Egyptian cotton with a tight weave. During wet weather the cotton would soak up moisture, swell and become waterproof, keeping the interior dry. Waterproof groundsheets fit the footprint of the tent and pockets running the full length of the inside, allowed storage for miscellaneous items. Impressively, even by modern day standards, a two-man tent weighed in at less than three and half pounds! Early one-piece tent pole designs, too long to be carried on a rucksack, were used in the same way as an alpen-stock. Later tent designs were equipped with brass-jointed bamboo tent poles and pegs cut from holly trees with a catch to hold the guy lines. Decorations in the form of flying Tyrolean eagles adorned the outside of some tents.

Woollen Jaeger blankets were transformed into sleeping bags with the addition of a zip. An unusual design feature was the ability for the bag's occupants to stand and walk. Detachable hoods, which could be replaced when necessary, increased the bag's comfort and warmth.

Rucksacks, made to order, could be bought in a variety of sizes, with or without pockets. Advertisements specified "Handicraft by a years user – Millican Dalton. Art green Willesden or brown proofed canvas, light, durable; broad, stiff web shoulder straps, adjustable, unhooking; with pole sling. Much superior to factory made: less bulky than Norwegian, third of the weight and half the cost."

Equipment was not only available for sale; it could also be hired. This was to be a great service to the public as not everyone had the funds to purchase and consequently the possibility of camping was opened to everyone, rich or poor.

Lightweight camping became a passion and was something he spent much time contemplating. It was known that he was very pleased with his achievements in reducing weight significantly into more transportable loads and much humour was had regarding his obsession with weight. Typically when camping in Wasdale he would purchase 1/2d sheets of stamps from the visiting postman which allowed him to send anything from a postcard to a parcel. On one occasion his purchase was greeted with the sarcastic comments "Yes, but think of all the extra weight you are carrying!" Regardless of light-weight camping equipment, climbing gear remained heavy and it was not uncommon for 200lb loads to be pushed to locations such as Esk Hause!

5
Professor of Adventure.

The High Lodore Camp sited above the Borrowdale Hotel. Derwentwater and Skiddaw in the distance. (Mayson Collection)

Choosing to operate in the north of the Lake District, the Borrowdale valley acted as the hub from which the locally known Borrowdale Hermit ran his business throughout the summer months. For many summers at the start of his new career, Millican pitched his tent and made camp at High Lodore above the Borrowdale Hotel on a grassy slope beneath the shadow of Comb Crags. This camp was the base for his camping tours and used by arrangement with the farmer at High Lodore Farm.

The High Lodore camp provided everything he could wish for – mountains, rock, water and a close proximity to Mother Nature. Dalton wrote about this camp in his article *A Camping Holiday:*

"One of my favourite camps is a steep fell side in Borrowdale, commanding a perfect view of a perfect lake, Derwentwater, framed by mountains on each side, with the purple bulk of Skiddaw in the distance; and I have watched many gorgeous sunsets from that spot, as we cooked over a wood fire and dined in the open. On one such occasion we reclined in our red blankets, gazing on the ever changing tints of the sky, yellow, orange, crimson, pink and grey, merging into the blue, purple and violet of the hills – all these colours duplicated in the lake beneath."

Although having made the choice to quit work as an employee, he decided to accept the position of Secretary for the Holiday Fellowship in the Newlands valley, where he worked for a season or two but unexpectedly soon found himself out of a job. Additional to the necessary administration duties associated with the position of Secretary, he was also expected to take guests out walking, but landed himself in trouble with the management after introducing them to rock climbing. Discarding the fact that he was working as a volunteer, these actions were seen as far too dangerous for novices and his innocent initiative earned him the sack.

Never one to be disheartened, the unsuccessful stint at the Holiday Fellowship was put down to experience and so he concentrated on his own guiding business. It is commonly assumed that Millican Dalton was the first Lakeland guide. On the contrary, by no means was Dalton the first mountaineering guide in the Lake District or elsewhere for that matter. In fact local shepherds acted as guides to the first walkers way before he was born. They had excellent knowledge of the mountains and knew of routes up rock faces prior to the advent of recreational rock-climbing.

As time elapsed and witnessed the decline of traditional Lakeland industries and the increase in tourism, it was realised that, with so many new faces visiting the region, the principle hotels should provide guiding services for their guests. In effect the outdoor scene had become so popular that up to the end of the nineteenth century fell guides were as well recognised in the Lakes as in Switzerland – although the numbers were somewhat less. Guides proved to be a major benefit to those guests who had insufficient confidence to enter the hills on their own.

One such guide emerged in Wasdale sometime around 1908. Literature from the Wastwater Hotel read, "A first class Dauphine guide and climber has been engaged, who will conduct climbers on the various climbs in the district at a moderate charge." Josef Gaspard, a resident guide employed by the season by Ritson Whiting, remained a regular at the hotel until the First World War. Summer saw his return home for the Alpine season where he also acted as a guide.

Gaspard pioneered no routes in the Lake District, but was by all accounts a competent climber, but as he tended to be busy teaching novices he did not generally venture onto the more difficult rock. Boisterous games in the billiard room, billiard fives and the traverse of the room using the walls and tables, provided entertainment in the evenings, but Gaspard never joined in with the other climbers or 'Tigers.' The 'Tigers' sniggered at the idea of a guide and considered Gaspard more of a servant; after all he cleaned the guests boots that totalled over 40 pairs on most occasions. Even before Gaspard's arrival the hotel had hired guides for decades. The hotel brochure for 1869 stated "Post Horses, Mountain Ponies, Wheeled Carriages, Boats, Guides, Post boys, Boatmen &c. always in readiness." In reality, early guides acted both as a porter and someone who could point out the right fell, leaving the rest to the "Gentleman Adventurer."

Necessitated by the increase in tourist trade was the formation of a work programme. Dalton, appearing to take his guiding business seriously, formed a programme that was generally drawn up at the beginning of the year and was thoroughly planned and co-ordinated. Dates in the programme could be reserved by individuals, groups or for club meets. Demand exceeded resources and many would-be clients were left in despair after hearing how his busy schedule would not allow him to be available for their trips. Each year's programme followed the same format so that winters could be spent in the south of England, several summer months in the Lakes and the remainder of his time distributed between trips abroad and other parts of the British Isles. A camping programme from 1913 read:

CAMPING TOURS
Through Lovely Scenery
ADVENTURES – NIGHT RAMBLES – BOATING – RAPID SHOOTING – BATHING-MOUNTAINEERING

Why not have your own real adventures and thrilling experiences, under safe leadership, and study Nature firsthand, instead of merely in books? Camping is a complete change from ordinary existence, and is undoubtedly the freest and healthiest mode of life, the fear of rheumatism is quite baseless, due precautions being taken. Among the many advantages over hotel or lodgings, the chief is perhaps that one is in the open-air in view of the ever varying aspects of the scenery, from getting up to bedtime – and even all night at times.

Select small camping parties (limited to 20) will be personally conducted by
MILLICAN DALTON
(Otherwise known as Robinson Crusoe, Buffalo Bill, Peter Pan, Sinbad the Sailor, the Wizard of the North, & Co.)
an expert mountaineer and camper well acquainted with the various districts.

ENGLISH LAKE DISTRICT
JUNE 22 – AUGUST 20
SEPTEMBER 27 – OCTOBER 11, 1913
PROGRAM

The address of the camp is: -C/o M. Dalton, High Lodore Farm, Keswick.

SAT. From Keswick Station, coach or walk four miles to the farm.
SUN. Quiet day about camp.
MON. Lodore Falls (pleasant scramble), Watendlath, Borrowdale, Bowder Stone.
TUES. Boating on Derwentwater; Shooting the Rapids; Bivouac on island.
WED. Sunrise Breakfast; Mountain ascent Scafell; Rock-climbing if desired; supper on mountainside.
THURS. Lazy day about camp.
FRI. Honister Pass, Buttermere and Crummock Lakes, Scale Force.
SAT. Helvellyn and Ullswater can be visited independently.
SUN. Walk round Derwentwater, by Castle Hill, Friar's Crag, Portinscale, Brandlehow; or quiet day.
MON. Mountain ascent-Great Gable-by most interesting route, passing the Needle and noted rock-climbs, which can be done if desired. Supper out.
TUE. Rafting on the Lake, bathing, picnicking.
WED. Greenup, Easedale, Grasmere, and Rydal. Bivouac overnight in open, or in cave if wet.
THRS. Windermere can be visited independently, before returning, via Dunmail Raise, Thirlmere, Harrop Fell and Watendlath to Camp.
FRI. Row round Derwentwater.

Special MOUNTAINEERING weeks will also be arranged, Sept. 27-Oct. 11.

Mountaineering is the best form of exercise; it uses all muscles, develops surefootedness, nerve and self-reliance, in an exhilarating atmosphere, amid scenes of grandeur not otherwise accessible. All the climbs are well known, and selections can be made to suit novices or experts. Climbing in the British Isles is perfectly safe under experienced guidance.

The Program is subject to modification by weather, etc, and is of course typical. It will be seasoned to taste with further real adventures and experiences such as the following: -

- Fording a Rapid River.
- Shooting the Rapids.
- A Dinner of the Savage Club on a Desert Island (temperature permitting.)
- A Sinbad the Sailor Act (write for photo card of this, price 2 1/2d
- Exploration of a Cave.
- Lost in the Mountain Mist.
- A Thunderstorm on the Mountains (weather permitting).
- Dangling over the Precipice.
- Astride the Razor Ridge (photo).
- Ascent of the Needle, Great Gable (photo).
- Climbing a Chimney (photo).
- Varied Hairbreadth Escapes (arranged by circumstances).
- Midnight row on Derwentwater, and Bivouac on island (photo).
- A Sunrise Breakfast by the Lake.

TERMS.

The full tour including two weeks camping, boating, mountaineering and meals £3

Camping, meals and walking excursions only, per day, 4/-, per week 25/-

N.B.-The 14-day return fare from London is additional 27/-

Less than 3 in a tent and more 'luxury' if desired, extra.

The food provided is simple but good and in quantity to cope with the camp appetite. The cooking is part of the gypsy experience and campers are expected to assist in rotation. This does not prevent anyone going excursions, but it can be escaped if desired by payment of 1/- per week.

VEGETARIANS are properly provided for.

Ladies are welcome to the camp. There is nothing new in ladies camping, the custom being at least 10,000 years old. One camping club almost contains 100 ladies.

EASTER.

A Mountaineering party will be arranged, the scenery and conditions at this time being similar, tho' on a small scale, to the Swiss Alps. Camp will be pitched at the foot of Scafell in the best climbing centre.

Cost inclusive of 12 mile drive from and to Seascale Stations, for the 4 days 35/-

Omitting the drives 25/-

Return rail from Euston 25/3

WHITSUN HOLIDAYS.
UP THE RIVER
Maidenhead to Sonning.

The combination of Rowing and Camping allows one to view the river under varying aspects from dawn to dark. A party will travel from Paddington to Maidenhead on Whit-Saturday afternoon, row up past the beautiful woods of Cliveden to Cookham and camp in a beautiful situation by a good bathing-pool. -Thence by Marlow and Hurley to Henley, and pitch on a wooded island below Sonning. -Monday back to Maidenhead, and London. A feature of this trip is the navigation of weir whirlpools and their rapid currents.

Charge including rail return fare, boat hire, all meals, lock fees and accommodation in the tents,
25/-
Friday evening to Tuesday morning 7/6 extra.
Week, Oxford and back 53/-
Ladies, 2/4 reduction.

Year after year for almost half century, Dalton retreated to the south of England for its milder winters and made a return to Borrowdale for the summer. On his reappearance he would create quite a stir. Local children would run around excitedly, repeatedly shouting "Millican Dalton's back! Millican Dalton's back!!…" To them he was like a movie star and regarded as a celebrity. To his friends his reappearance meant the chance of more adventures and days on the fells, but to the tourists it meant the opportunity to be guided by the man who was developing a reputation as a leading light.

Conceived by many as an all round expert, his wide ranging and mastered skills earned him the impressive accolade of Professor of Adventure, a name which he was very fond, to him a name more significant than a knighthood. "Among my friends I am known as the Professor of Adventure and during the summer months I conduct parties on expeditions" said Dalton.

6
Robin Hood or Robinson Crusoe?

Dalton – The inventor of shorts? (F.& R.C.C. Collection)

Millican's change in lifestyle brought with it a whole new freedom of choice and the opportunity to dress as he wished, not forgetting that Victorian fashion was of a uniform nature. Early in his new life he clothed himself in traditional shirts with trousers rolled up to the knees. This soon changed though and his appearance became most distinctive, differing greatly from that of the day, making him instantly recognisable. People who saw him spoke of similar descriptions. First impressions varied from a rather tattered scoutmaster to a veteran of the Boer War, whilst others thought he looked similar to Robin Hood or Robinson Crusoe. Resulting from his unorthodox appearance were many nicknames ranging from Rob Roy and Peter Pan to Wizard of the North, to name but a few. Distinguished not just in clothing but also in stature, he stood clear of the crowd and was head and shoulders above most, a tall and thin man well over six foot tall who moved with long, strong strides.

To compensate for life on a minimal income, he adopted cost cutting exercises and began designing and manufacturing his own clothes with the use of his sewing machine. Fashion reforming designs, simple yet strong and efficient, tended to be a dull olive green or brown. For one reason or another the clothes never seemed to be finished and never hemmed, simply turned up at the edges. Always alert for things for free, he would keep a keen eye open for discarded fabrics which he could use in his manufacture of clothing or camping equipment – canvas, sail cloth, oil skins, string and rope.

A Tyrolean theme, chosen for whatever reason, was the basis for his designs. Upon his head was a large Tyrolean hat that became his trademark. It was practically worn all the time and was clipped up at the side and decorated with a feather. On one occasion the brim of the hat was held in place with what looked like a huge ruby, but which on closer inspection turned out to be nothing more than a red reflector from his bicycle! A sprig of heather sometimes complimented the decorative feather.

The rest of his attire consisted of an old khaki or green jacket and shorts. The shorts, commonly made of corduroy, exposed a pair of much discoloured and chapped knees. In fact his legs were so tanned it was difficult to distinguish them from his shorts. The shorts, were quite long and more often than not rolled up – except when climbing when they would be ingeniously unrolled to protect the knees and he wore them every day without fail, rain, snow or sunshine. Below the shorts a pair of old army puttees covered his calves. These long strips of cloth; coiled around the leg from ankle to knee, provided protection and support.

Dalton was adamant that he himself had invented the pair of shorts as opposed to the commonly perceived Robert Baden-Powell, hero of the defence of Mafeking and founder of the Boy Scout movement. In reality neither was responsible for such an invention. Uniforms of the South African Constabulary and Army consisted of shorts well before Millican Dalton and Baden-Powell thought of them. Interestingly though, it is true to some extent that both men had some involvement in the introduction of short trousers. Baden-Powell sent a letter to the parents of boys inviting them to the first scout camp on Brownsea Island on 25th July 1907 and used the word 'shorts' in the camp kit list. Shorts at that time had not become a familiar fashion concept and only worn in hot climates principally by soldiers. Long trousers or knickerbockers were all the rage.

Existing photos of the Brownsea Island camp however, show none of the pioneering boy scouts in shorts. Baden-Powell used the term 'shorts' again in the first part of *Scouting For Boys* (1908) as part of the 'ideal Scout uniform.' Maybe Baden-Powell introduced shorts as a fashion concept for young people and by including them as part of Scout uniform became popular garments. Fashion was not on Dalton's agenda and so, perhaps, it could be claimed he introduced shorts as functional sportswear.

A red Scotch plaid added a touch of colour to his otherwise plain clothing and had two uses. Primarily it was used as a shawl, but when cold weather approached and temperatures dropped, the plaid served as a blanket to beef up his sleeping arrangements. On occasions the plaid also acted as an improvised sail for his rafts. Curiously the majority of the Dalton family used plaids, possibly indicating a Scottish family connection. Further to the Scottish link is the fact that Millican was regarded as a 'Wallacite' by friends and therefore, presumably, an admirer of Scotland's heroic liberator and worldwide symbol of freedom, William Wallace.

On his feet he wore handmade leather boots finished with Clinkers and three headed Tricouni nails, generally without socks. A comfort item to most, socks were detested and avoided whenever possible. Life was free, easy, careless and more often than not bootless, preferring to walk around camp barefoot. Lightweight sandals became a more comfortable option and sometimes worn in preference to the heavy, sturdy nailed boots. On the rare occasions that socks were worn, foot cloths, pieces of cloth covering the heel and sole of the foot, prevented premature wear and the need for darning repairs. Coloured cloth, generally blue, tied around his ankles also prevented scree from entering his boots.

Dalton was a smoker, a chain smoker to be precise and never seemed to appear without a Woodbine which he kept in a small tin box. All strenuous activities would be undertaken with a cigarette in his mouth, pausing frequently to light another and he would consume each smoke as though inhaling oxygen. Whether a genuine lover of smoking or nicotine dependant, after starting he was unable to quit. Evidently a cigarette was needed before he could function properly as they helped build up steam! As a rather strange sight to some guests, Dalton frequented the public bar of the Borrowdale Hotel once or twice a week to buy Woodbines in fives. Standing out from the crowd somewhat, in his Tyrolean gear, against the backdrop of wood panelling and formal wear, intrigued the guests who looked on with great interest but never scorn. He did not hang around though and rarely talked or mixed with the hotel guests. On occasions his clients were made to wait outside whilst he made his purchase. Yellow smoke stained fingers and whiskers showed that he enjoyed plenty of them. "I hadn't better say anything about the tobacco habit. It's a bad habit, isn't it?" confessed Millican, "But we must have some creature comfort. And cigarette smoking is difficult to get rid of. Perhaps. I do smoke rather too many cigarettes."

His beard, an abundance of magnificent Victorian style facial hair, was sported in the form of a ragged goatee beard that had turned grey early in life. Occasionally the pirate beard was reduced to a moustache.

Bright blue eyes contrasted with his permanently tanned face, which some say, looked like leather. Whether the glow to his skin was acquired through endless time spent outdoors, or through a lack of soap and water, general cleanliness was not a priority and not always practical. A culmination of smells from body odours, wood smoke, tobacco and general outdoor living was, apparently, quite off putting and accordingly advice was to stand well upwind!

Regardless of the lack of hygiene, camping outdoors did not mean that all home comforts had to be neglected. Actually, he refused to rough it and was adept at achieving comfort wherever possible. Sleeping arrangements, although Spartan, made for satisfying nights sleep. His mattress was a springy bed of dry bracken upon which he slept rolled up in the "wondrous comfort" of an eiderdown quilt. When necessary the eiderdown was beefed up with the Scotch plaid and one of his intense, long burning fires kept temperatures around the immediate area above freezing.

In fact he was a little too accustomed to sleeping in the outdoors, which became more than obvious during a visit to an aunt's house. It was arranged that he was to spend the night with the family and, having made up his bed, the aunt thought he would be comfortable, but could not believe her eyes after Millican complained that the bed was too soft and dragged the bedding forthwith onto the floor where he spent the night!

Dalton's unorthodox homely appearance unfortunately became a subject for mockery amongst a minority of small-minded individuals who sneered at his homemade clothes. Undoubtedly aware that his self-styled Tyrolean image singled him out, he seemed unconcerned with other's attitudes and was more interested in his own affairs. Whether or not some thought he looked strange, he was one of the outstanding 'sights' of Keswick and as a result his image and services became well known enough to be used as model for the Keswick Boot, as sold by boot maker Frederick Birkett of 2 St. John Street, Keswick. He sold "Boots and shoes, specially suitable for the district, made to measure on the premises."

The Keswick Boot, made by Fred Birkett and promoted by Millican Dalton.

Reflecting his curious outward appearance was his curious inner self. Dalton was a charismatic and instantly likeable person whose honesty, natural modesty, absence of self-seeking and unselfish nature, made him many friends, though it must be admitted that there were others who disliked him. As a man of education and culture, he possessed excellent communication skills that allowed for dealings with people from all walks of life, grades and calibre. Highly intelligent, adaptable and very opinionated he could hold a conversation on a vast range of subjects. However, the unusual, confident and sometimes forceful expression of his views sometimes raised eyebrows.

Although choosing to close the chapter on city life and step out of mainstream society, it did not mean that a silence had to be maintained. Quite the opposite, he would not hesitate to voice his opinions, either verbally or in writing, to whoever it concerned and whatever their position in society. Politics with a particular emphasis on war and peace was one such issue that stirred strong emotions. Socialist tendencies and leftwing views concerned with social and economic justice befitted his frugal approach to life.

Funding this frugal existence was purely through Millican's own means, but nevertheless, handling money on a day-to-day basis was deemed unacceptable as it meant enduring the problems associated with it. Greed and capitalism formed no part of his philosophy. For obvious reasons he had to deal with money for food and provisions, but that was about all. It was common for him to refuse payment for his services in the form of cash, but would gladly accept gestures of appreciation in the guise of cigarettes, food or newspapers. "In long association, I never knew him charge anything for his services beyond a trifle for camping expenses" wrote friend Mabel M. Barker. Amazingly, at one point he even refused payments of interest on his savings, to the astonishment of the Post Office. It is possible that the thought of receiving interest payments contradicted his socialist ideals. He was determined not to be a capitalist.

Maintaining a positive attitude and always looking on the bright side enabled Millican to always see the advantages in getting up and doing something whatever the weather. Hour after hour was spent examining his surroundings. Particular enjoyment was found exploring mountain and rock with a rucksack, coffee and food, stopping to brew whenever and wherever he felt the urge. Indeed remnants of his fires dotted the landscape, most of which were simply used to make coffee. His get-up-and-go attitude did not however, mean that he rushed. On the contrary, life was taken at a laid-back pace and he was never known to rush. He was contented to do things in his own time, well aware that there was nothing to hurry for.

7
Dietary Values.

Tea by the River: Millican, Jean Brown and Mabel Barker, September 1935.
(Mabel Barker Collection)

Campcraft, the art of outdoor living, was an indispensable skill and was studied as part of Dalton's curriculum, forming a major element of all camping holidays. He possessed years of knowledge and through carefully explained lessons, the newcomer could learn the expertise of the professional camper. His students very quickly learnt the choicest locations to camp, the vital positioning of tent or bivouac, and the creation of bedding and fireplaces. With a hands-on approach to teaching, the construction and lighting of fires, their management and development for either warmth or cooking became clear. Highlighting of the correct choice of fuel, from kindling to logs, was ensued by enlightenment in outdoor fare and the adaptation of recipes for use on an open fire.

Cooking over real flames was considered the only way to prepare food and nothing was substitute for a good old-fashioned wood fire. A gift of a portable primus stove by an unknown woman proved to be rather unwelcome, as being from the old school of thought no way was this sufficiently traditional or enough fun to be utilised. The clean, kerosene burning stove was demoted to the corner of the tent where it was knocked around before being discarded.

Every person taught by Dalton soon became acutely aware of his dietary ideals. "I use only the barest necessities of life and am a vegetarian" he said and on another occasion cited "I'm a vegetarian and live mainly on wholemeal bread I bake myself." From what is known he never publicly explained the reasons behind his vegetarian beliefs, but they could possibly have related to simplicity and economy. Although abiding strictly to these beliefs he was never seen to preach his opinions and remained open minded.

Homemade bread, baked to his own recipe using wholemeal flour, formed his staple diet. Wholemeal bread is in fact the 'staff of life' for most vegetarians and was also the cornerstone of Dalton's diet. He really did use only the barest of necessities and told one visitor to his camp "Use is everything. We dress too much, we eat too much, almost everything we do is too much. Put a man to it, and see what he can put up with." Sure that it was possible and well aware that a billion people live on rice alone with no nutritional deficiencies, he emphasised "The Chinese live on rice, so why can't we live on bread?" He was right to surmise that the ingredients in his bread could maintain a healthy body. His mix was heavy, coarse textured, unrefined bread, packed with goodness and flavour. Highly fibrous, high in proteins, carbohydrates and iron and fundamentally filling – it certainly was a meal in itself. In reality though, Dalton did not live on bread alone, but still appeared to avoid all luxuries.

Baking was a technique which had been mastered, a skill made all the more impressive as it was all done without the aid of a conventional oven. Not only did he bake bread, but also rudimentary oatcakes and occasionally 'fancy' cakes as a treat for guests, again made to his own recipe. Indeed much pleasure was had in acting as host and he was equally happy to cater for friends, clients or even strangers to whom he passed on, but never forced, his dietetic ideals.

He was adept at catering for large groups of people and it was obvious that campfire cuisine was a speciality. Routine menus, always simple, altered little except for seasonal variations. Benefits of a vast knowledge of food for free allowed for fruitful pickings. As a keen amateur botanist, food stood out and was not searched for in the common sense of the word. He knew the places to look, things to pick and what to avoid. The lushness of the Borrowdale valley produced copious amounts of fruits, nuts and edible plants. Hazel nuts, which grew near the River Derwent, were according to Millican some of the best he had ever tasted, apparently being at their best quality in autumn. Berries growing wild along the lanes, on lakeside, riverside, hillside and on the valley floor were all put to use, raspberries, blackberries and bleaberries to name but a few. Sometimes the addition of nuts and berries to the bread dough further increased its taste and nutritional value.

The result of his efforts was plain and humble but tasty and wholesome food. However, not everyone could stomach the modest culinary offerings, proving too unpalatable for some would-be diners due to unintentional additions of ash and cinders, which somehow found their way into the billycan! This was a true eye-opener for many first time campers new to camp foods, who were familiar only with homemade food.

Not all foodstuffs could be foraged from the land and so shopping trips still had to be undertaken. When resident in the Lake District, trips to Keswick or Plaskett's Store in Rosthwaite were made on his trusty bicycle. Supplies such as oats, wholemeal flour and coffee, commonly listed for purchase, were obtained from J. S. Allinsons, grocer and provision dealer, 25 Main Street, Keswick, who offered "Everything of the best at the lowest prices." As a rule he only bought raw ingredients from which he could make his own meals, proving to be the most cost efficient method. In contrast, whilst in the south, he fulfilled the role of subsistence farmer. Befitting the frugal approach to living was the small-time cultivation of his fruit and vegetable garden. Allowing for a virtually free source of food, the warmer Essex climate provided ideal husbandry conditions, yielding ample harvests of freshly grown crops.

Recognising the value of food and the need for a well-fuelled body and healthy appetite, he commented "After you have been on the fells all day you can eat anything that is plain and wholesome though, of course, you can eat a whole lot of it." However, it was not just essential to feed after a day on the fells, but just as important before the day's activities began. After all 'you are what you eat' and if an energetic day was to be had, a good start was in order. Each day, without fail, commenced with breakfast and generally consisted of what Millican referred to as "parched oats" – dry fried oat flakes, roasted in a pan. The roasting, traditionally a Dalesman technique, added some flavour to the normally bland taste. Water was then added to form porridge into which syrup was drizzled to sweeten the mix. "For breakfast I have porridge," said Dalton "I put the meal into a frying pan and partly roast it before I add the boiling water. I am a bit of a sweet tooth and I serve it with syrup."

During the day Brazil nuts, stored in his pocked, were snacked on whilst out and about, especially when climbing, to help maintain high energy levels. Evening meals of bread, more often than not accompanied by boiled vegetables, concluded the day's intake.

In an early form of recycling it was found that, as a matter of course, he could supply himself with all the kitchen equipment needed from Grange tip – or any tip for that matter. Grange tip, on the opposite side of the River Derwent to Cummacatta Wood, was a happy hunting ground for Dalton. Indeed, he proved the point that one man's rubbish is another man's treasure. Ever alert for things for free, such treasure was salvaged and put to all sorts of uses. Discarded food tins and pots, to which wire handles had been added, provided cooking vessels of differing sizes. Gadgets of all descriptions, devised with the help of a good imagination, assisted in the preparation and cooking of food. Rustic instruments such as tongs, sculpted from suitable lengths of wire, saved burnt fingers. Reclaimed barrels and empty bottles made the imperative transportation and storage of water easy.

However, fresh water, a plentiful commodity in the Lakes, was not always too easy to find. On a broiling day in the middle of summer Dalton and a friend found their water bottles had run dry whilst wandering the high fells in the vicinity of Scafell Pike. Parched and in desperate need of a drink, they began to hunt for water. Although close to the wettest spot in the country they were distant from all visible watercourses and no water was to be found, even though the previous week had witnessed heavy rain. The friend was close to giving up the search when Dalton remembered "Come on. I know where there is water!" Leading the way to a nearby weather station, he opened the door, and withdrew the rainwater gauge. Without delay the thirsty duo quickly emptied the receptacle of its handsome volume of water. Presumably, the meteorologist was flabbergasted after climbing several thousand feet to find nothing to measure, bearing in mind the recent downpour.

From the age of 11 Millican was well aware of problems associated with alcohol and seemed to maintain his pledge with the Band of Hope, even in adult life. In preference to alcohol was a heavy consumption of very strong, black coffee that was, after smoking, Millican's only other luxury and vice. "The only recipe for making good coffee is to use plenty of it. I never boil the coffee. I bring it three times to the boil, but never boil it. That's a drink fit for a connoisseur. I can drink coffee all the day long" said Dalton. Syrup was again used as a sweetener; so much was added that some said a teaspoon could be stood up in the brew! Becoming rather famous for coffee, his adoration for brewing-up was referred to as his "ruling passion." During times of inclement weather cup after cup would be knocked back in anticipation of a settled spell. Freshly baked bread and brewed coffee flooded his camps with a delicious urbane aroma.

Surprisingly, the apparent unfaltering abstention from alcohol was said to have hit a stumbling block when Dalton was out with Ralph H. Mayson, Bill Ireland and a Mr Barron. Whether through his own choice or through trickery, Dalton succumbed to the intoxicating effects of drink in the bar of the Royal Oak Hotel, Station Street, Keswick. After the session the merry group staggered to Mayson's Emporium on Lake Road, where it was suggested Dalton was to have his portrait taken. On entering the studio he took position in front of the printed studio backdrop, dressed in breeches, waistcoat and jacket, barefoot with a stick and sat low down on a wooden chair, capturing the drunken moment.

With the exception of alcohol the consumption of this sufficiently varied, vegetarian diet satisfied all food classes. It was a nourishing, vitamin enriched and high fibre diet. Evidence was in his claim to have never suffered from a common cold and he was sure that diet and the outdoor life increased resistance to illness. "I never have a cold," said Millican.

8
You're My Rock.

'Climb = 8000ft!' (Mayson Collection)

The pioneering of new routes is the ultimate achievement for the majority of climbers and, it seems, Millican Dalton was no exception to the rule. In 1897 Millican, Andrew Thomson and 'E. R.' grasped their own piece of history and recorded an official first ascent on Doves' Nest Crags in the glacial hanging valley of Combe Ghyll. An initial exploration of the Borrowdale Fells the previous year by Thomson and others from Kendal, had led to the discovery of the crags, but it was only on returning with Dalton that the pioneering attempt was apparently made. Bentley Beetham, generally perceived as the pioneer of Borrowdale, described the area in the 1953 F.& R.C.C. Borrowdale Guide:

"The place is quite unlike anything else in the whole of the Lake District: it is not, as it is sometimes said to be, the result of ancient mine or quarry workings; it is a rare natural phenomenon. A great rock face of a buttress has slipped bodily forwards and downwards; but instead of crashing into scree at the base of the cliff, its fall has been arrested, and it now leans back against the cliff from which it came, leaving cavities and fissures between the detached blocks and the parent rock. It is the 'subterranean' character of the route through these fissures that has made Doves' Nest so widely known. The exploration of the dark passages is interesting; the work is a pleasant mixture of potholing and rock climbing. On account of the sinuous and intricate nature of the routes in both vertical and horizontal planes they are as difficult to describe as they are to follow, and Doves' Nest must be one of the few places in Cumberland where a guide, i.e., a leader who really knows the terrain, is of much value to a party."

If any guide was of value on these crags then it had to be Dalton who, without exaggeration, knew Doves' Nest better than anyone. It was a favourite place to experience adventure with a difference, where he climbed not only with parties and friends, but also, more often than not on his own. To prove his unrivalled knowledge of the crag he wrote several route descriptions for the *Fell and Rock Climbing Club Journal* 1914 including a description of the route pioneered with Thomson and 'E.R.' which they named South or Buzzard Chimney:

The Fell and Rock Climbing Journal
Volume 3 – Number 2 – November 1914

DOVE NEST
By MILLICAN DALTON

The wonderfully splintered collection of problems on this little crag deserves the attention of more climbers than it obtains. On its discovery some 18 years since by the late Andrew Thomson and other Kendalians, the place was felicitously described by them as the "rock gym."

Specimens of nearly every variety of rock climbing are to be found here within a space of 150 feet square – a pinnacle, faces, hand and "stomach" traverses, chimneys galore, with, in addition, an excellent substitute for a pothole.

The crag is situated opposite Raven Crag in the great hollow of Glaramara, and can be reached in three-quarter hour's ascent from the Borrowdale road. Opposite Mountain View the lane for Thorneythwaite Farm leads to a gate, and a path there branches to the left and winds upwards to the marshy floor of the Combe. Crossing the streamlet a sheep track leads to the crags.

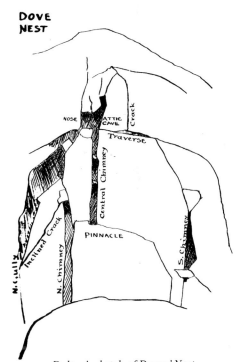

Dalton's sketch of Doves' Nest.

The most interesting routes on Dove Nest, good enough for expert parties, are as follows: -

SOUTH, OR BUZZARD CHIMNEY – Commence with back on left wall, using

Climbing on Doves' Nest Crags. (F.& R.C.C. Collection)

minute footholds on opposite wall. Twenty-five feet of pure back and knee chimneying brings the chockstone into reach. A bight of rope should then be threaded through, so that it provides a secure hand-hold, whilst completely reversing the body. The crack on the left of chockstone can then be utilised to complete the pitch. Above the chockstone the route leads up steep incline to left to the traverse. The second man should belay at the left of the traverse, whilst the leader finishes up a vertical crack rising halfway along. The first ascent was made by M. D., A. T., and E. R. in 1897.

On my second ascent of the chimney I got into rather an awkward predicament. When threading a rope-end under the chockstone, I allowed insufficient length and found myself checked unexpectedly when endeavouring to surmount the chockstone. Not at all relishing any descent, I clung on whilst the situation was discussed with those below. Andrew Thomson finally came to the rescue by climbing an easier route to the top of the chockstone, whence he slung down a noose to me; slipping into this pitch.

CENTRAL CHIMNEY – A good approach to this is over the ridge of the Pinnacle, thence descending into the chimney foot. The difficulty of the chimney varies according to whether it is climbed well inside, or nearer to the open. At the top of the pitch is the Attic cave, with a bleaberry patch at its entrance. A long stretch and stride above the chimney takes the leader to the foot of a difficult crack in rather a sensational situation. A careful study of the problem is desirable before stepping off the bleaberry patch to attempt the crack. At the top of the crack a move onto the buttress finishes the difficulty. Hitches for the rope are available at foot of the crack and whilst ascending it.

THE INSIDE CAVE – On walking right into the south chimney, an arrow drawn on the rock indicates the concealed entrance. As the cave is quite dark, artificial light is necessary, such as an acetylene lamp with hood removed, or an alpine lantern will serve.

36

String for suspending the light comes in useful at places, and a supply of matches should also be carried. Continuing forward inside the entrance brings the explorer to a black chasm, about 30 feet deep. The easiest way to reach the bottom is along a ledge on the right-hand wall to its further edge, whence descent is not difficult. The return to the entrance can be made by traversing the chimney at a lower level than the ledge, or by climbing up a vertical hole.

From near the entrance a weird climb of 80 feet, towards a glimmer of light, leads into the attic cave and the open air again. A higher and more difficult exit can be reached by continuing the ascent before emerging into daylight. During the ascent the sensation may be heightened by throwing

Belaying on Doves' Nest Crags. (Mayson Collection)

blazing newspapers down the dark abyss! As sound is magnified in the confined space, sensation produced by contact between sharp projecting points of rock and the human head should be carefully avoided!

The descent can be made either by the Central Chimney, or by the North Gully. At the foot of the latter, round a corner to the left looking down, is the interesting Inclined Crack leading upwards: and from the top of this, the Pinnacle can be reached by a short descent down a crack, and a swing on the arms across North Chimney.

In addition to the routes aforesaid, sundry problems can be solved:-
- Short inclined crack on right wall of North Gully.
- Traverse diagonally across central slab from foot of South Chimney.
- Chimney on North of Pinnacle.
- Chimney on East (inside) of Pinnacle.

The Stiffest problem is the Nose, at the top of North Gully. It has only been done by one party, about 8 years ago, Percy Salter and the late Tom Rennison. Being more difficult that the Pillar Nose direct, with very minute and insecure holds, almost as hazardous for follower as for leader, a second ascent is not recommended.

For the novice an interesting run is – over the Pinnacle, into Central Chimney, down North Gully, and through a tunnel to North Chimney: thence down behind the Pinnacle.

"One often hears" continued Beetham, "that Doves' Nest is the place to go in wet weather, and though it is true that by doing so you get out of the rain, it does not follow that you get out of the 'wet,' for water may be found dripping from the roof and streaming down the walls and onto unskilfully shielded candles. It would be better to say that however bad the weather is you can still put in an enjoyable day there."

This was definitely the case for Dalton who visited whatever the weather. In fact he began to spend so much time there that he adopted a disused corn mill as a temporary base, which, being only a short distance from the crag, offered the only real protection during inclement weather. Increasing the mills appeal further was the provision of a pot-bellied stove. Grimble, Dalton's friend, also frequented the mill on occasions.

'Round the corner from Dove Nest.' Millican (right) and Grimble under shelter in a disused corn mill.

As with the pioneering developments in the Lake District, Snowdonia in Wales also witnessed an explosion of interest in rock climbing in the late 19th Century. Excellent and varied climbing throughout the region was said to be as good as anywhere in the world and therefore became a base for many early pioneers. As pioneering climbers themselves the Dalton Brothers, Millican and Henry, also frequented the area where they set out to establish their own climbs. Over time, Millican's efforts were noted and considered to be a good reason for membership to the Climbers Club. Millican, proposed by J. W. Puttrell and seconded by Ashley Perry Abraham, both original members, was eventually elected as a member on 14th February 1902. Not long after his election he attended the fifth Annual Dinner, which took place after the Annual Meeting. The Dinner took place at Café Royal, Regent Street, London, on Friday 9th May 1902 at which about 40 members attended. Subsequent Annual Meetings and Dinners were ignored.

After extensive exploration and camping expeditions in the Welsh wilderness, the brothers recorded a first ascent in 1903 on Craig Cau, located amidst the beautiful landscape of the Cader Idris area. The route, located on a remote northeast-facing cliff, rose dramatically above the dark sinister waters of Llyn Cau and terminated beneath the summit of Mynydd Pencoed. It was called Pencoed Pillar, a gigantic 740 feet HVD (Hard Very Difficult) three star climb, considered a classic amongst classics. Botanical scrambles past Alpine flowers, greasy grooves, good holds, stances and belays constituted to this great mountaineering route of considerable character and breathtaking exposure. Heavy vegetation practically made the route unclimbable during wet weather with conditions only becoming favourable after several dry days and; in effect, distinguished the climb as a summer route.

An account of this climb appeared in *Rock Climbing in North Wales,* written by George and Ashley Abraham in 1906 and read:

This magnificent bastion of rock forms the left-hand retaining wall of the Great Gully. Its north ridge presents a terrific precipice which borders on the vertical in its upper part. When Mr Jones told us in 1897 that it had never been climbed up this side, he made a statement, which holds good even at the present time and will probably go down to posterity with equal accuracy. Jones had said "See that fine buttress on the left of the gully? That's Pencoed Pillar. It has not been climbed, and I doubt if it ever will be, up this side."

Several strong parties have looked at it from below and passed on; others have essayed its ascent, leaving no record of their failure. In June 1903, however, Messrs M. and H. G. Dalton discovered a somewhat circuitous route up the Pillar which "compares in point of difficulty and interest with the Great Gully." I am indebted to Mr M. Dalton for a few notes on their climb and for indicating it on the outline drawing of Craig y cae. They started from the grass terrace. By the way of steep heather-covered rocks, they mounted rapidly until the ridge of the Pillar became almost vertical. An overhanging rock "which might have been surmounted had they possessed an ice axe" turned them back, so they retraced their steps until able to traverse upward to the left wall from the Great Gully.

Passing the foot of a chimney which seemed to lead back to the ridge, but which looked exceedingly difficult, they came to a milder looking one heading in the opposite direction. The lower part of this they ascended with difficulty and then traversed out to its left wall, which they scaled "by the aid of friction holds." Steep, bleaberry covered slopes were then followed until a practicable traverse to the right disclosed itself. This enabled them to regain the crest of the ridge, about 200 feet above where they had left it, whence they easily gained the top of the Pillar. They describe the traverse as "extremely impressive." At one point they had to cross the head of an incipient gully, gaining its far wall by means of a hand traverse, one hold on which consisted of "doubling the fist in a crack."

It sounds pretty lively, but if its difficulty be not greater than any encountered in the Great Gully the climb is to be recommended. They explored the ridge for some distance downward, leaving about 150 feet still untouched by climbers.

Many years later George Abraham wrote in his book *British Mountain Climbs*, 1923: Those genial pioneers of real, British mountaineering camp-life, Messrs Millican and Henry Dalton, discovered a route up the Pillar but mostly on its easterly side. The presence of much vegetation and the possibilities of numerous variations will militate against the climb becoming popular. For whatever reason Dalton's subscription to the Climbers Club was relatively short lived; and after almost four years as a member he resigned on 31st December 1905.

Adding to his climbing credentials, although not pioneered, was the Matterhorn (4478m) in the Pennine Alps on the Swiss-Italian border that he successfully climbed sometime between 1905 and 1914. Edward Whymper may have conquered the Matterhorn decades earlier, but due to the lack of technical advances the route was as difficult as ever with Dalton using the same equipment and similar clothing. This impressive Alpine mountaineering achievement highlights his nerve and skill, suggesting that he was a more than experienced climber. Intriguingly, considering his Alpine mountaineering ability and interest in the sport, he never became a member of the Alpine Club, formed in 1857 and based in London.

9
The Fell and Rock Climbing Club.

Grange Bridge, Borrowdale. Dalton second from right. (F.& R.C.C. Collection)

Recreational rock climbing had reached its twentieth year when a couple of friends evolved the idea of forming their own climbing club. Edward Scantlebury suggested to friend, Alan Craig, who with others travelled to Coniston every Sunday fell walking, that they should form a club. It was after the two enthusiasts had read Owen Glynn Jones's inspirational book, *Rock Climbing in the English Lake District*, that they took up the sport of climbing and as a result of their exploits believed it was a sufficiently good cause for the formation of a club. As two members were insufficient they roped in Chas Grayson, G. H. Charter and S. H. Gordon who frequently joined them on their way to Coniston. These five, the real originators of the club, formed a committee of themselves complete with secretary and treasurer – but it was to Scantlebury that the club owed its existence. Gathering in the Sun Hotel, Coniston on the 11th November 1906 for the club's first meeting, with the exception of Gordon who joined a little later, they discussed the aims of the club. A suitable name, chosen after much debate on a previous occasion, led to the creation of the "Fell and Rock Climbing Club of the English Lake District."

Primary aims of the Club included the promotion and encouragement of fell walking and rock climbing within the Lake District and to act as a bonding link between its members. In order to achieve these aims the Club organised climbing meets at various key locations. The Sun Hotel, Coniston; Wastwater Hotel, Wasdale Head; New Hotel, Dungeon Ghyll, Langdale; Jopson's Farm, Thorneythwaite, Borrowdale and Buttermere Hotel, Buttermere constituted the Club's official quarters. Climbing books kept at each of these quarters acted as a log for climbers to record details of their efforts. Annual club dinners provided a social aspect off the fells and the publishing of an annual journal high-lighted new route developments and featured articles submitted by members.

In an attempt to attract new members from a wider audience the distribution of circulars detailed the Club's existence and within a few months membership stood at almost 200. First President, Ashley Abraham, added great impetus to the club in the early years with credibility of the F.& R.C.C. assured when the legendary father of the sport W. P. Haskett-Smith, the renowned Solly and respected Cecil Slingsby added their names to the list of members.

In spite of Dalton's friendship with several Kendalians and other climbers from south Lakeland he was not a regular to the Coniston area and was only really friendly with one committee member – H. B. Lyon. Regardless of Lyon's status as committee member, Dalton did not become a member himself until his return north from Billericay around Easter 1907. Although it is improbable he would have been a founder member it is highly likely that, had he been resident in Cumberland at the time of the Club formation, he would have been in the first wave of membership applicants and even one of the original 13 ordinary members. Subscription for the first year of the Club was purely nominal with the second and subsequent season's subscription being somewhat increased – consequently 14 members resigned.

Without doubt Dalton was already a competent climber way before the concept of the F.& R.C.C. and did not join as a novice. He was however, keen to be involved, he wanted to be part of the action and wasted no time in participating in the Club's activities.

F.& R.C.C. archives, currently held at Kendal Records Office, suggest that Millican's first Club outing was the Club Meet at Seathwaite in Borrowdale between the 3rd and 7th August 1907. It was not as well attended as anticipated despite the fact that Chas Grayson had previously notified all members by postcard. Attending members, only eight in total, included H. B. Lyon, Andrew Thomson, Chas Grayson and Edward Scantlebury. The first day was ushered in with much rain, so the eight members staying at Jopson's Farm amused themselves in the morning by making first ascents up the barn wall into the hayloft. An hour or two was beguiled in the loft with hay climbing, obstacle races and wrestling. After dinner, the weather slightly finer, they took candles and a lantern from the farm and made a start for the caves on Doves' Nest Crag.

During the course of the week the group climbed popular routes of the day and managed to scale Napes Needle, Eagle's Nest Arête, Kern Knotts Chimney, New West, Slab and Notch and finally Pendlebury Traverse. On the 6th August Dalton and Lyon split from the main group and made a return to Pillar Rock. Miserable, wet and misty weather did not hamper progress and the double act managed to reach the summit via New West descending by East Jordan.

Pillar Rock was also the destination the following week, this time with the Bottrerills, the Seatrees and a couple of other friends and yet again headed up New West. Several weeks later the journey from Borrowdale to Langdale was undertaken for the first Langdale Meet. Gimmer Crag and a new route pioneered by a fell and rock party, including Dalton, proved to be the highlight of the Meet. On the 22nd September the

'On the way to Gimmer.' A Fell and Rock party in Langdale. Millican Dalton (front row, second from right) attached by rope to his cousin T. J. Rennison (Middle row, second from left). (F.& R.C.C. Collection)

group claimed a first ascent of Junipall Gully, a moderate graded climb. With no pause for breath Dalton was off again making a return to the north Lakes and visited Pillar Rock with P. R. Shannon and J. R. Rennison for a Sunday outing on the 29th September, ascending North Climb to the summit and descending via East Jordan.

Strong gales and mist-covered fells spoilt any good intentions of climbing on 8th June 1908 and so hiking took precedence. Departing early morning from Coniston, A. Gregson, W. Gregson, Chas Grayson and Dalton headed for Brown Pike, Coniston Old Man, Great How Crags, Carrs and Wetherlam. "The mist lifted and turned very nice later on," wrote one of the climbers in the Coniston climbing book.

It was almost a year before Dalton ventured on his next Club Meet to Coniston on 4th and 5th July 1908. A turnout of quality climbers included the Keswick Brothers, Ashley and George Abraham, G. M. Thorpe, G. C. Turner, H. B. Lyon, C. H. Oliverson, A. R. Thomson, Edward Scantlebury, A. Craig, Chas Grayson and Percy Suller. Climbs on the agenda featured Great Gully, Intermediate Gully, North Gully, Woodhouse's Route and B. Buttress.

Jaunts were made to Pillar Rock many more times over the subsequent years after his first visit, originally with friends and in later years guiding large parties of up to a dozen people (Sunday April 16th 1911). Evidence of his fondness for Pillar Rock exists in the numerous entries made in the green climbing book, housed in a weatherproof container on the summit, used for recording routes, climbers, weather conditions and dates.

The 1912 F.& R.C.C. Borrowdale Meet commenced on Sunday 18th August, but Dalton did not join the group until the following day when eight members climbed Kern Knotts Chimney. It was somewhat of a quiet meet – Dalton did not participate in any other climbs and in fact the entire group abstained from climbing on Thursday 22nd when they all tramped over the fells to Grasmere Sports via Easedale.

In the first few years of the Club's existence Dalton wrote two articles and a small submission for inclusion within the Club's journal. The first, *A Camping Holiday*, high-lighted the benefits of open-air life. The second, *Dove Nest*, detailed various routes and acts as the only historical evidence of his first ascents in Lakeland. A write-up for Bowder Pinnacle (now known as Bowderstone Pinnacle), pioneered by friend Ralph H. Mayson, also featured within *Climbs Old and New*:

Climbs Old and New – Fell and Rock Climbing Club Journal 1914.
Bowder Pinnacle, Borrowdale.

On the crag from which the Bowderstone traces its descent there is a pinnacle which yields a good climb. The pinnacle, with a chimney on its left, can be picked out from the road below. A traverse leads from the gully on the right, and thence upward the foot of a wide chimney, which is climbed by the back and foot method to the top of the pinnacle.

The pinnacle can be left (or approached) by a very long awkward stride across the chimney to another ridge, from the end of which a short climb up by a yew tree brings the climber to easy slopes. I think Fred Mallinson and Ralph Mayson were the pioneers. M.D.

༼ ༈ ༽

Although rock climbing was still a relatively new sport, certain routes, being more popular than others, had felt the burden of large volumes of traffic and become increas-ingly littered. Concerned about the state of these climbs several F.& R.C.C. members planned a conscientious cleanup expedition to Walkers Gully on Pillar Rock in 1912.

Their primary purpose was to collect abandoned climbing rope, which had been left behind for a multitude of reasons. Not only was this a blot on the landscape, it also hindered the progress and enjoyment of other climbers. Millican Dalton, W. B. Brunskill, H. G. Dale and H. B. Gibson set out on the climb only to be overwhelmed by the amount of gear to remove and gave up the attempt around the third pitch with their rucksacks full. A much disintegrated packet of sandwiches at the foot of the top pitch, a capacious ruck-sack, two rock climbing guidebooks and a lady's waterproof were, amongst other items, removed from the gully. One member of the party was so interested in the waterproof that he tried it on and although finding it comfortable to wear was apparently a little tight around the waist and shoulders!

Over the years the number of F.& R.C.C. members rose dramatically and the club almost became too popular. This also applied to the crags to some extent. The once quiet Club Meets began to develop into mass excursions to the mountains. It was not uncommon to have to wait in turn for many minutes, even hours, on the popular routes during a busy meet. This was not Dalton's style. Whilst enjoying the company of up to 20 people or so, the thought of larger crowds did not appeal to him and, according to Club archives, he never appeared at a Club Meet in the Lake District again after 1915. Crowded Annual Club Dinners, the highlight of the calendar for many members, were also held in a similar disregard and shown by a persistent non-attendance. Even the Club Dinner of 1928, held at the Windermere Hydro, Bowness-on-Windermere, could not lure Dalton, despite celebrity guest speaker Hugh Walpole, the Keswick based author, taking centre stage. Clearly Dalton desired to do his own thing and ensured that he did.

Some years after his last Club Meet appearance, in the autumn of 1920, a number of enthusiastic F.& R.C.C. members who lived in the south of England gathered together and discussed the validity of a London Section. Members living in the north questioned the need for a London Section, but after highlighting the difficulties and expense of long distance travel and the post-war slump, which necessitated an ever-increased curtailment of weekend jaunts to the Lakes, consideration was granted. After several unofficial gatherings it was decided, with the blessing of the Club, that a London Section was warranted and should be created. Consequently the Section was formed at the end of 1920 with its main intentions to provide monthly outings into the countryside, an outlet for keeping fit and the opportunity for members to talk about all things mountainous. Committee Member W. P. Haskett-Smith was probably the most notable member of the London Section.

It was during the 1921-1922 season that Dalton rekindled his affection with the F.& R.C.C. and became a member of the London Section himself. Soon after joining on 2nd November 1921, he was included in a Section foray to Welwyn. Of the group, several members decided to head north towards Ayot St. Lawrence. With Captain Hetherington-Brown acting as spokesman they visited George Bernard Shaw's house, but he was not at home. The Irish playwright was much admired by Millican Dalton who he considered to be one of the few sensible people in the world. This may come as a surprise considering that Shaw tended to provoke rage and dislike in his younger years through his scandalously subversive opinions and, in his later years, the strong indications that he sympathised with Stalin, Hitler and Mussolini – but no one, including Dalton, disputed his genius. In fact they shared much in common. Shaw admitted he was not suited to work and could not abide the restrictions of being employed. He was a strict vegetarian, enjoyed walking in the Ayot countryside and respected all living things as equals. Both men had a deep concern for humanity, leftwing views and intellectual originality. Continuing the common link was Shaw's opposition to the wars and his active protests against them.

February 26th 1922 again saw a London Section outing, this time to Chingford. The party was keen to enter Epping Forest and did so at the earliest opportunity. On their way to High Beech Dalton suggested that tree climbing could be an option, but the damp weather thwarted his plan. After exploring the depths of the forest the group stopped and ate a soggy lunch before setting off for Almesbury Bank. Debate between the knowledgeable members focused on whether the forests British encampment was in fact raised in AD 60 by Queen Boudicca. At the end of the outing Dalton offered to provide tea. Most accepted but several found themselves so engrossed in the topical discussions of Everest and oxygen that they ended up lost but nevertheless managed to meet the rest of the party at Chingford Station.

In future years the number of London Section members rocketed and as a result, sometime in the 1930's or 1940's, his membership was left to expire.

10
The Epping Camp.

After several years spent at "The Camp" in Billericay it was decided that a change of scenery and a return to his childhood roots was in order. Over the years, Epping Forest, due to its accessibility and resources for adventure, had become a favourite area to camp. After all it was the Dalton brothers first training grounds where their voracious taste for adventure was born. Every inch of the forest had been explored, from ancient earthworks and ponds to coppices and former roads; all the darkest recesses were known. Around 1910 the 15 mile journey west was made, where he followed in the footsteps of many other like minded people before him and set up camp in Epping Forest. Proving to be ideal surroundings, the forest was not only a huge expanse of almost ten thousand acres in which it was easy to escape, it was still convenient for shops, transport links, friends and family.

The Epping Hut c. 1925.
M. D. stitching a rucksack.

Sometime in the region of 1900 his spirited Cumberland mother and youngest brother, Henry, had moved from Highams Park to 226 Hale End Road, Hale End, Woodford Green, Essex; also known as 1 Elm Villas. Meanwhile, Joseph had married and bought a house down the road at number 149. He, unlike Henry, had progressed on from the world of insurance and was by now County Examiner of Stamps. Although welcome to stay at the family home, Millican maintained his alternative lifestyle and preferred to spend his time in the outdoors at his Epping camp. In fact, the only benefit of his mother's house to him was not the security of a roof but the postal address, which was used for several seasons as a contact address for his guiding 'business.'

Prior to the Epping Forest Act 1878 the forest was a similar situation to Thornwood and Billericay in the fact that many gypsies, hawkers, vagabonds, hermits and men of the road camped within its boundary. The Act was commissioned by the City of London Corporation to govern Epping Forest as Conservators. Upholding a duty to ensure that forestland remained unenclosed and preserved for the enjoyment of the general public was the primary mission. Preservation of the natural aspect of the forest through protection of trees, other plants and the ancient earthworks, prevention of wood cutting and the removal of earth and resistance to new construction on forest land constituted the Acts mission. Forest Keepers, sometimes referred to as Woodmen, were assigned to enforce compliance with the Act and to ensure that such damage to the forest was prevented. Therefore as the majority of travellers caused much destruction and disturbance, they became looked upon with great disregard. Their wish to live in the forest was refused and they found themselves moved on, with their dark barrel tents and carved and painted caravans on a regular basis.

Curiously though, a close friendship with the Forest Keepers allowed Dalton to camp in the forest unhindered and regardless of the Epping Forest Act it was rumoured that he was probably the only person allowed to light fires by special arrangement. Unfortunately, finer details of the deal in which they would turn a blind eye to his activities are uncertain.

Although originally consisting of only a tent the encampment, located on the edge of the forest, soon took on different guises. In need of something more substantial the tent was superseded by the comfort of a small wooden hut, which was similar to a garden shed. It was constructed from overlapped timber and featured a hinged door, an internal fireplace and was equipped with everything he needed – bedding, cooking utensils, food, books, pens and paper. His library of books, journals and photographs was available to both visitors and passers-by alike. It has been suggested that at one point the Epping camp comprised of a strange treetop dwelling of his own devising, which must be assumed to be some form of tree house high in the canopy.

Hospitality was provided and although a simple affair he would share everything and was more than pleased to offer coffee and food to anyone. Treats for guests included merry singsongs, jovial parties around his fire and constant servings of tea and coffee. Letters, photographs and tree "boling" also provided entertainment. All new ascents were named and the favourites climbed over and over again. Dalton was well known in and around Epping Forest. He was a well-respected character amongst local residents, Forest Keepers, colliers and other woodland workers, with whom he was particularly famed for his love of tree climbing.

As a result of his reputation he was happy to teach folk the techniques associated with the construction of tree-houses, bivouacs, rope ladders, swings, bows and arrows and the skills involved in tree "boling" and tracking to anybody who wanted to listen. Such enthusiasm for teaching was unheard of and the opportunity to experience innovative and daring escapades soon got him a following.

Changing seasons brought with them new and diverse challenges. During the winter months the forest was transformed into a crisp, white, winter wonderland creating even more resources for fun and adventure. Undeterred by the warning signs posted around the many ponds signifying: *Danger! Thin Ice,* he would be the first to don his crudely fashioned homemade wooden skates and glide effortlessly across Baldwin's Pond and the like. And when the thaw set in and the 'rinks' were nothing more than slush he would be the last to take them off. Dalton was a most impressive and natural skater whose balance was insurmountable, but which was fine-tuned with the aid of a cigar, which was humorously claimed to assist! Even more impressive were his long, handmade skis with which he zipped down the gentle slopes of the forest. Visits to the Alps had introduced Dalton to this hairbreadth sport and, as a particularly rare sight in Essex, mesmerised the local youngsters, especially the boys.

Life in the forest was not all fun and games. September 1914 brought with it the Great War (1914-1918) that immediately curtailed the efforts of many climbers. Some were involved in one of the armed forces, some volunteered and others had priorities away from the sport. At the age of 47 Dalton was too old to fight and, as an ardent pacifist, would have refused anyway. Irrelevant to the lack of threat posed to mainland Britain from invasion, the southeast still experienced the first Zeppelin air raids, such as the one over nearby Loughton. Choosing not to retreat to the safety of the Lake District until the end of the hostilities he decided to live his life as normal and defiantly persisted in travelling between Essex and Cumberland to meet up with friends for climbing holidays.

Irrespective of his non-participation in the conflict, the war still had a direct affect. A bizarre incident occurred in the autumn of 1914 in which Police arrested Dalton under the suspicion of being a German spy. Whilst going about his own business at the Epping camp, a hiker, who had spotted him and become suspicious of his motives, informed the police. When they arrived on the scene Millican was perched in a tree dressed in his usual attire. This must have looked suspect as the police ignored his innocent claims of being a camper and subsequently detained him. He eventually appeared in the dock before Woodford Magistrates Court where it took the efforts of several friends and reliable witnesses, who took the stand in his defence, to have the charges dropped.

Eventually fire destroyed the Epping hut in which his collection of photographs, letters and early volumes of the *Fell and Rock Journal* were lost. Laid-back as ever Dalton made light of the situation and simply commented that at least he would not have to bother replying to the letters!

11
My First Leader.

'Our camp in Borrowdale' – Madge, Mabel and Millican September 2nd 1919.
(Mabel Barker Collection)

In 1913, after hearing of "Camping Holidays, Mountain Rapid Shooting, Rafting, Hairbreadth Escapes," a lady by the name of Mabel Mary Barker wrote to Dalton regarding the hire of tents and equipment. Barker, acting as leader for a party of students from Saffron Walden, Essex, was proposing to camp at Seathwaite, Borrowdale. George Morris, mutually friendly with the two of them, had told Mabel about Millican well before they ever met during a discussion on literature. "I know the original of the chief character in Rest Harrow" Morris told Mabel, "At least, he is like enough to have suggested him." Apparently Dalton had tried to lure Morris onto the rocks without success.

Dalton, ever keen to help out in his area of expertise, was only too pleased to provide the tents. One evening he made his way from High Lodore and visited the Seathwaite camp to check on the welfare of the 25 or so female party members, known by Barker as the "Walden Gipsies," and the performance of his equipment. "Then and thereafter" wrote Mabel "He reminded me of pictures of Robinson Crusoe. He made his own clothes, very strong and efficient, and entirely of his own design, and of a dull green,

'The Walden Gypsies – 2nd week, The Tribe.' (Mabel Barker Collection)

toning with the fells. But whether from choice or a streak of laziness (I do not think I ever saw him hurry) they were never quite finished, the edges remaining unhemmed."

Later that evening, after dark and with campfire lit, he took position and, without fail, set up a billycan arrangement and brewed-up forthwith. "He was at home throughout his life by any camp-fire; certainly so at mine" added Mabel.

During the course of the holiday one of the "Walden Gypsies" had boots that required mending. Forever offering assis-

Dalton with rucksack and tent,
Seathwaite 1913.
(Mabel Barker Collection)

tance, Dalton took them away to Plaskett's store in Rosthwaite. Unfortunately the shop had closed for the day, so trustingly he left them on the doorstep. To the astonishment of the students, who doubted his better judgement, they returned in due time safe, sound, repaired and ready for use.

The two of them maintained a friendship and joined forces later that year after he had quite casually offered to take any one of them climbing, "I could hardly believe my ears" exclaimed Mabel. Arriving at Needle Gully in some force on 31st July 1913, Barker and her group prepared for a day on the rocks with their newly discovered friend. This was when climbing officially started for Barker, the fells and rocks being the original and abiding link between them both. Napes Needle, an impressive introductory ascent, was her first roped attempt on which she took second behind Dalton's lead.

Dalton and Barker hit it off straight away, she was somewhat like him – rather unconventional, well educated and possessed a love of nature and the outdoors. Dr Mabel Barker, Litt.D., B.Sc. gained her geography diploma at Oxford and her B.Sc. in geology in London. At her home in Friar Row, Caldbeck she maintained an organised mess of masses of books, papers and photo albums which enveloped her living space. At one point she rescued an injured Jackdaw that became a domesticated pet named Johnnie. Generously hospitable, she would share anything with anyone and whilst at home would keep a pan of broth on the stove for the benefit of lucky and hungry hikers who would tramp past her door.

Only a week after their first roped climb some of the same party met up with Dalton

again and, feeling more confident, tackled the problems on Kern Knotts. This proved to be their last climb of the season and a further twelve months elapsed before they happened to meet up quite by chance in September 1914 when Mabel and friend, Norah Geddes, were walking the Borrowdale Fells. His eagerness for non-stop adventure led them both by "glimmering and guttering candles" through the caves on Doves' Nest. It was on this climb that Mabel was "greatly impressed" to note the seat of his shorts to which had been sewn a

Dalton and Barker ascending the Needle, 31st July 1913. (Mabel Barker Collection)

Dalton and Barker on top of the Needle.
(Mabel Barker Collection)

large patch of Willesden canvas to keep his rear dry whilst seated! Norah Geddes, incidentally, was the daughter of the distinguished Scottish Renaissance man, Sir Patrick Geddes, ecologist, town planner and botanist. Patrick Geddes employed Mabel for several years. (For some time prior to the Great War she assisted Geddes at Edinburgh University and in future years supported him again at the University of Montpellier where she achieved a doctorate for her French thesis on education.)

Eagle's Nest Ridge and Arrowhead Ridge finalised the summer's climbing before the interruption of the Great War, which temporarily ended the Dalton-Barker climbing partnership.

Meanwhile, April 1913 had brought with it the death of Frances Dalton. Chronic bronchitis ended her life at the age of 80 years whilst at home at 1 Elm Villas. The surviving brothers Joseph, Millican and Henry, all included in the resulting Will and Testament, received approximately £700 each which incorporated a

Dalton, in the centre of the photograph, on Kern Knotts August 1913. (Mabel Barker Collection)

share of the legacy of their late grandfather, Tinniswood Millican. Following her death it appears that Millican moved into 8 Lincoln Terrace, Loughton, sited on the outer limits of Epping Forest adjacent to Woodbury Knoll.

With the Great War well underway Dalton, as a conscientious objector, thought there must be a peaceful solution to the conflict. Pacifism was a subject, which stirred strong emotions from within, so much so in fact that his disagreement with the government's actions during the conflict was clearly evident in a correspondence to Mabel. The letter, dated 14th June 1915, sent from his home at Lincoln Terrace stated "I wonder when, if ever, the British government will have sense to propose peace." Pacifism, literally 'making peace', is a core Quaker value and, although not technically a Quaker, he was raised by their beliefs. The vast majority of Quakers are pacifists and it is probably an exception to find a Quaker who is not.

Mabel's camping exploits, in addition to her climbing, were also cut short and the France trip appears to be her last for the duration of the war. Subsequently, she travelled to Holland to assist the Society of Friends with the escalating refugee crisis. Ensuing the war she returned to lecture in London and later taught at King Langley's Priory, Hertfordshire. Whilst working there she began making weekend visits to Epping Forest to join Dalton and other friends where they climbed trees, discussed the chances of the early Everest expeditions and occasionally visited his forest hut.

With Lincoln Terrace facing demolition, Dalton was forced to move again and settled in one of several cottages clustered around the Foresters Arms on Baldwin's Hill, Loughton. After the dawn of the 20th century it would seem that Loughton, as with many areas north of London, developed into a sanctuary from the mushrooming conurbation. Loughton was indeed a quiet retreat with the population, even as late as 1921, standing at a mere 360 people. Artists, freethinkers, wealthy merchants and assorted intellectuals were particularly attracted to The Hills area, primarily due to its close proximity to Epping Forest. A common non-conformity adopted by these residents in terms of religion and outlook was particularly apparent. Residents, including Jacob Epstein amongst others, although not remembered individually, contributed to a wider revolution in popularising arts and crafts and a display of sympathy for the workingman. It was in The Hills area that Dalton's home, Walnut Cottage, was located in a small row known as Stony Path. Immediately adjacent to Stony Path was the forest boundary, allowing for unequalled and unrestricted access. It was this close proximity to nature, it seems, that was essential and even with the luxury of Walnut Cottage, he continued to camp and bivouac in the forest, satisfying his preference for the outdoor life.

Further post-war excitement and the return of normal life revived the Dalton-Barker climbing partnership and in 1919 they scaled Walla Crag and Mouse Ghyll, both situated just outside Keswick. At this point she did not have any other climbing partners and Millican was her only contact with the rope throughout her first years of climbing.

Around the same time, Millican visited Friar Row. Concluding a lengthy evenings discussion it was arranged that he was to stay overnight to save the homeward journey in

8 Lincoln Den
Loughton
Essex
14/6/15

Dear Miss Barker

With reference to your letter, my program having been made up some time ago, I am sorry that it wont be possible for me to be free for France — The Devon Camp is a fixture for a club & runs to Aug 21 — after which I have some other people booked for the Lakes —

If the reconstruction scheme goes forward successfully I should be pleased to arrange to supply any camp equipment — as to which I gave Miss Geddes a detailed list some months ago — This is I suppose accessible to you?

I wonder when, if ever, the British government will have the sense to propose peace —

With kind regards
Yours sincerely
Millican Dalton

Dalton's letter to Barker. He is clearly in favour of a peaceful solution to the Great War.

darkness. Mabel knowing his unorthodox choice of sleeping arrangements and not wanting to be insulting was not sure whether to offer him the best bedroom, the garage or a tent in the garden!

Clearly Dalton was never far from all things unconventional, so it is of no surprise that he was best man in the strangest of ceremonies when Mabel's brother, Arnold and fiancée Madge Owen married later that same year. Mabel had originally introduced Arnold and Madge and so both were friendly with Millican. Desiring, for one reason or another, a service with the minimum of fuss but still in a church, the couple carefully chose to conduct their wedding at St Andrew's Parish Church, Rosthwaite. Throughout the run up to the big day the four met on a daily basis. A couple of Dalton's friends from his office days had also travelled to join in the fun and were, in

'Best man congregation!' Dalton with friends from his office days at Shepherd's Crag, 15th September 1919. (Mabel Barker Collection)

effect, the best man congregation. On the eve of the ceremony Madge and Mabel camped out at High Lodore between Grange Fell and the Borrowdale Hotel.

Meeting in the morning of 16th September the quartet headed for Rosthwaite looking more comparable to a climbing party than a wedding congregation. Abandoning the tradition of morning dress and white wedding gown, the bride and groom opted for the comfort and practicality of tweeds. Millican was in complete climbing costume, boots, rucksack and rope and most uncharacteristically a pair of socks. Apparently he endured with the discomfort of the socks until the end of the service, but on emerging from the quaint church he sat down and removed them immediately! A quick photograph was followed by the wedding reception held at a cave used by Millican on the flank of Castle Crag.

The Happy Couple, centre, with Mabel and Millican, September 16th 1919. (Mabel Barker Collection)

The 'wedding breakfast,' prepared and cooked with an open mind, by Dalton a staunch vegetarian, befitted the simplicity of the occasion and consisted of a chicken boiled in a billycan. Sporting activities concluded the Happy Couple's day with all enjoying an afternoons climbing in and around the nearby quarries. No records exist for these ascents.

"I had a few more days with him on the fells" wrote Mabel, "strange it is, on looking up dates, to realise how very few and precious they were, and how far spaced." Their

'Wedding Breakfast Cave.' September 16th 1919. (Mabel Barker Collection)

'Sports after wedding breakfast,' September 16th 1919.
(Mabel Barker Collection)

days together were indeed far spaced and a further two years passed before their next meeting during a camp at Taylorgill Force – a fine foaming cascade at the head of Seathwaite – when Dalton led a small party including Mabel in 1921. The famous blue bicycle again acted as a porter's trolley and transported the majority of their gear past Seathwaite Farm to the foot of the Force where they made camp. The camp, adjacent to the Sty Head packhorse route, was convenient for the high fells and crags such as Scafell Pike and Great Gable. Whilst exploring the area a member of the group stumbled upon a stash of tinned food hidden deep in grass and boulders. Rusty and without labels, it appeared that the tins had been long forgotten about. Claiming the stash as their own the campers proceeded to excitingly open the tins to check their mysterious contents. Unfortunately for Millican, most contained meat orientated foods, so the majority of the spoils went to the others.

Mabel's climbing ability and confidence had gained in leaps and bounds since her first roped climb. It was later in the summer of 1921 that, in addition to climbing Doves' Nest, Eagle's Nest Chimney and Needle Ridge, she undertook her first lead – Kern Knotts Chimney. On another occasion that summer Ralph Mayson accompanied Millican and Mabel to Great Gable and climbed Napes Needle, Kern Knotts Buttress and Eagle's Nest Direct. As Barker had become a good friend, competent climber and lover of the sport of climbing, Dalton and Mayson talked openly about proposing her for membership of the F.& R.C.C. (Rule number five – "All candidates for membership must be proposed and seconded by members of the Club, and will be elected subject to the approval of the Committee.")

"That same season" continued Mabel "joined by Coward of Keswick, we did the climb now called Black Crag Buttress, but then Troutdale Buttress; and on another day had some fun on the Ennerdale Face of Gable. For the first (and most certainly the last) time, I was inveigled into that detestable affair called Smugglers' Chimney. Dalton, very knowing about it, kindly gave the lead to Coward. Then he went round to the top, and sat there making sarcastic remarks about how long we took and '*Snugglers*' Chimney, while we fought and gasped in what should really be called '*Strugglers*' Chimney."

Sometime in 1922 Mabel joined the F.& R.C.C. She had blossomed into an accomplished climber and had outstanding ability at a time when only a few women ventured onto the crags. What she lacked in physical strength was made up for with her exquisite style. Without doubt, Dalton was fully confident in Mabel's ability and was happy to let her take responsibility. She wrote "When we climbed together it was rather a shock to find that I was expected as a matter of course to take the lead."

Despite their close relationship they apparently never became more than friends. In fact her favourite companion was C. D. Frankland. They may not have exactly been in love but they enjoyed each other's company and spent significant time together camping and climbing. In 1925 Frankland led Mabel up Central Buttress on Scafell Crag. This was the hardest route in the Lake District and up until their ascent had only been climbed three times before, but more importantly it was the first ever ascent by a woman. The next year, again with Frankland, she became the first woman to traverse the Cullin Ridge on the Isle of Skye and years later in 1936, aged 50 also became the first woman to descend Central Buttress.

In future years Mabel developed arthritis, which prevented any further climbing; it also signified a premature end to the Dalton-Barker climbing partnership, but they remained friends. "In all the later years, up to the outbreak of the last war (WWII)" added Mabel "we met from time to time." During and after WWII they maintained their friendship by post.

12
Safe and Sound.

Publicity shot or bad technique? (Mayson Collection)

It was the general opinion in certain sections of the climbing community that Millican Dalton was rather over cautious and lacked the ability and nerve of the 'Tigers.' Modern day critics suggest he routinely disregarded client safety and failed to use belays.

Whilst climbing for different reasons than most, his ability and nerve was every inch that of the 'Tigers.' He climbed the same routes in and around Wasdale and also pioneered new routes. Chronologically he was not far behind the recreational pioneers of the 1880's and had claimed a first ascent when the sport was still only 11 years old.

The very concept of searching for new routes to pioneer differentiates some climbers from others and elevates pioneers into a league of their own. Unknown climbing on virgin rock and the lack of knowledge of the next move or the crux dissuades many, who prefer to follow in the steps of others. Pioneering requires nerve and an element of skill in reading the climb, noticing it in the first instance and belief that it can, more likely than not, be climbed to the top. Dalton's first ascents of Doves' Nest and Pencoed Pillar are prime examples of such nerve and skill. His route description for Doves' Nest outlines climbs suitable for experts and, as one of the routes is his, it becomes apparent that he considered himself an expert.

Seemingly unconcerned with fact, these uneducated opinions discount the many years of experience gained by climbing both on the continent and in the British Isles. Even in the early days new techniques could only be adopted as and when they became introduced. Equipment used was no different than the choice of other climbers. He employed the same nailed boots, pure Manila hemp Alpine rope and a long wooden shafted ice axe which was utilised to 'garden' routes (clear vegetation and debris) and was an integral piece of kit essential on virgin rock or unpopular routes.

Contrary to these misconceptions he was actually a very safe climber who never took unnecessary risks, especially when guiding and was, by all accounts, rather cautious. Understandably as a guide he would never put clients, who were under his duty of care, in any danger and would not take a novice on any climbs that were beyond their physical or mental capabilities. Under no circumstances would a novice be allowed to take the lead.

Additional to teaching the basics of balance and movement he also passed on his knowledge of safety, demonstrating the use of belays and how to tie knots correctly. Showing the safe length of a pitch, he would indicate practicable methods to care for the leader and the general safety of the whole party.

If anything, his unhurried, methodical and simplified approach ensured that students really did absorb his knowledge, increasing the safety aspects of his tuition. Dalton was an extremely patient and natural teacher whose encouraging manner allayed fear. Questions, more than welcome, received answers in a cheery tone – precise and clear explanations relieved nervous beginners. Folk, young and old, of differing abilities and aptitudes, sought his enlightenment and all were warmly accepted on his courses.

Millican possessed the lightest of touches and handed down his skills to many first-rate climbers. One time student Mabel M. Barker was probably the best British woman rock climber in her own time. She had full faith in his teaching abilities and wrote, "I was never really happy in the use of any knots but his…Probably, by modern day methods (1947), he was overcautious, but it's a good fault…He was not ever, I think, among the great climbers. He had no ambition to be so. In a way he had no ambition at all."

In light of these misconceptions a full programme was always maintained and he attracted no adverse publicity. Climbers within the F.& R.C.C., undisturbed by hearsay, also trusted their own judgements. Accomplished climbers Ashley and George Abraham, Edward Scantlebury, Chas Grayson and seven others climbed with him on 4th and 5th July 1908 at the Coniston Meet suggesting he was a contemporary.

These unfounded allegations of bad practice are based on the misinterpretation of a promotional photograph that depicts an unsafe belaying technique supposedly with a client in tow. Upon first sight of this photograph, if unaware of Dalton's ability, a prejudice could easily be formed. Nevertheless this photograph, taken by Ralph Mayson, was nothing more than a publicity shot with Dalton 'posing' for the camera. In reality no client existed. Had he been bringing up the second he would have most definitely belayed by threading the rope around a chockstone or used a bight of rope around a spike of rock.

Important to the defence of his reputation is the highlighting of the Keswick boot image. Immediately recognised as the same location as the postcard there is, intriguingly, no rucksack and he appears in a seated position. Would he really have belayed from such an awkward and ineffective position? Other poses on this pedestal, possibly only a matter of feet from the ground, complimented the available collection of Professor of Adventure postcards. Some images were even inverted to achieve an alternative perspective further confirming the photograph as a stage-managed publicity shot.

Talk of accidents occurring under his guidance was unheard of. This was an excellent safety record considering he guided hundreds, if not thousands, of people throughout his long and eventful career – something that could not be said for all Lakeland guides. However, whilst climbing in his free time he pushed himself to the limit and occasionally surpassed his capabilities. A reporter investigating for the Sunday Chronicle in 1933 was told by Dalton "I have had many hairbreadth escapes from death. Once while on a rock climbing expedition I slipped, and but for the prompt action and presence of mind of another member of the party I would have been dashed to death."

Upon realisation of Dalton's priorities it becomes apparent that climbing was a passion and as with everything else in his life, was only for his own benefit and not for that of others. It is because of this that his skills as a cragsman should not be underestimated and it is more likely than not that he had a more substantial influence on the British climbing scene than was first realised. As a commendable achievement well worth highlighting, South or Buzzard Chimney, Doves' Nest, was only the sixth recorded first ascent in Borrowdale. Only the Abraham brothers, O. G. Jones, W. C. Slingsby, J. W. Robinson and a couple of other climbers had earlier recorded ascents in the valley. As a matter of course it was common for Dalton not to record first ascents. Climbing and having fun with friends was more important than claiming a first, indicating a distinct lack of self-glorification. Interestingly, South Chimney, Doves' Nest, was not recorded officially until 17 years after the pioneering climb when he wrote a route description for the *Fell and Rock Journal* of 1914. Other variations on this route purportedly pioneered by Dalton were never recorded.

More interesting still is the fact that a further 24 years passed before the accomplished climber Bentley Beetham made his mark in Borrowdale with Woden's Face Original Route in 1921. Incidentally, only five other routes were recorded between 1897 and 1921. Apparently the explorative instincts and zest shown by Beetham necessitated a separate Borrowdale guidebook. Until his appearance on the scene the number of recorded climbs in the valley were few and far between and therefore grouped with the more comprehensive Great Gable guide. The F.& R.C.C. Guide to Borrowdale 1953, written by Beetham, contained 131 of his own routes. The Editor's note asks why, considering Beetham's "astonishing efforts," Borrowdale was overlooked when Keswick, being of such close proximity, offered easy access to the rock for the many competent climbers who lived there. Moreover, the Editor states that Beetham could claim, without exaggeration, to have almost created a new climbing ground. It is a fact that the majority of early climbers frequented and concentrated on areas around Wasdale Head. Few ventured to Borrowdale specifically to climb due to its distance from the popular and challenging cliffs abounding Great Gable and Pillar Rock. Even those who passed through Borrowdale, purportedly, ignored the few 'credible' climbs amongst the dearth of exigent rock. In theory the Abraham Brothers should have more routes credited to them in Borrowdale, but found themselves busy climbing in Wasdale, concentrating on more difficult rock and their professional photography.

Shepherd's Crag, between the Borrowdale and Lodore Hotels, was supposedly one of Beetham's finest discoveries. Lying only 100 yards from the road the crag affords the most easily accessible rock in the whole of the country with stunning views to match. Yet, according to Beetham, because the crag is immediately disguised by a band of trees and lush, green vegetation, droves of climbing parties had walked parallel to it completely oblivious to its existence for 36 years since the sport began in earnest. Shepherd's Crag, it seems according to the guidebooks, was not discovered until 1922. Beetham along with climbing partner C. D. Frankland, returning to Keswick from Wasdale, caught a glimpse of a spur of rock that looked appealing. After an initial investigation they climbed it and thought no more of it. This route was named Brown Slabs Arête.

Without detracting from Beetham's admirable achievements it is of great surprise to learn that, remembering his explorative instincts, a return to Shepherd's Crag was not made until 24 years after his first visit when he eventually noticed the far better standard of climbing to the south of the crag.

Of great significance, and a total contradiction to Beetham's claims on Shepherd's Crag, was Dalton's visit to the south of the crag in September 1919, 27 years before Beetham's discovery. Dalton, photographed with friends from his office days is clearly seen taking tea dressed in climbing regalia, nailed boots and with an uncoiled rope slung over his shoulder, appearing to be taking a break from climbing. He was not on the south of the crag looking for Scotch mist, neither was the rope for decoration. In fact his achievements on Shepherd's Crag may never be fully realised, but in reality preceded Beetham to this "new climbing ground." Thinking logically, Dalton, based on the slopes of High Lodore Farm for many years, could not have missed the south end of the cliff.

Similarly with most other crags in the valley and knowing Dalton's taste for adventure and exploration it seems highly improbable that he pioneered no other routes in Borrowdale. Imagine, for example, passing the cliffs on the Borrowdale Road, would Dalton, an avid climber, have cycled past and not made an attempt? It was well known that he was happy to potter about and must surely have explored? Would he have travelled high over the fells and ignored all? Would he have called himself the Professor of Adventure if he only stood back and watched from afar? Borrowdale was his base, the hub from which he operated in the Lake District. Dalton was not merely a fleeting weekender or day-tripper, but a seasonal worker whose time, both free and working, revolved around the outdoors, with a particular emphasis on climbing. He was a mountain man; mountains were his life to which he had devoted everything. Anything that looked like a mountain was deemed fair game and he wanted to climb it. It would be fair to say that he knew the fells as other folk know their own street.

In reality, scores of climbs were discovered, inspected and attempted with successful achievements unrecorded. Obviously such records are at the discretion of the pioneer and act as the only real proof, but maybe, Millican Dalton could have been the true pioneer of Borrowdale!

Climbing was so appealing to Dalton that he was rumoured to have once been travelling through London along the Embankment with a friend quite contently when upon passing Cleopatra's Needle, Dalton stopped and looked up with a twinkle in his eye. With a good idea of what Dalton was thinking the friend urged him to continue their onward journey and the opportunity of a remarkable first was apparently forfeited. Unlike many he would venture out on the rock on his own and on the off chance of a passer-by, would shout down "Can you tie a bowline?" encouraging them to tie on and climb with him.

Favourite climbs amongst his personal repertoire included Scafell's: The Keswick Brothers' Climb, Slingsby's Chimney and Moss Ghyll. On Great Gable: Arrowhead Ridge, Eagle's Nest Ridge, Abbey Buttress and West Chimney; Doves' Nest and its caves at the head of Combe Ghyll and in Langstrath, Gash Rock, Sergeant Crag Gully, and the bouldering problems of the Woofe Stones which he delighted at. Of all the climbs in Lakeland his favourite was without doubt Napes Needle. So popular was this climb that

he scaled it well over fifty times. To celebrate his fiftieth ascent in style he carried a pile of sticks to its spectacular and exposed summit with which he made a small fire and brewed some coffee. Apart from his usual consumption of Woodbines he had an extra smoke with his freshly made coffee to celebrate his achievement. For each subsequent birthday after the event he returned to the summit of the Needle for a brew and a smoke in the same fashion.

On top of the Needle, as seen from Needle Ridge, 1913. Wastwater in the distance. (Mabel Barker Collection)

13

The Tirol.

Brewing up at 11500 feet. (Mabel Barker Collection)

Whilst at the Epping Camp in 1919 Dalton and Barker had discussed the possibility of a continental holiday. Barker suggested that she would organise a group if Dalton chose the objective and acted as guide. Post Great War Europe was a devastated place, but one which had witnessed vast reconstruction. Tourists began to return and financially the strength of sterling against foreign currencies made for cheaper travel and therefore provided a means for many to visit continental destinations. As agreed, the plan came together with the Austrian Tirol – The Zillerthal the choice destination with intentions to stay for a month. Mabel sure did organise a group with 30 people enlisted on the expedition, a party ranging from small boys to middle-aged women.

The party departed from London's Victoria station and caught the train destined for Dover, making the journey in reserved carriages. Millican, unconcerned with paperwork, left the clerical side to Mabel who was responsible for the distribution of passports and tickets. They left Dover and after a lovely Channel crossing arrived at Ostend and continued their rail journey across the Belgium countryside in daylight, leaving at 4pm. Due to problems at the Belgian-German frontier the party had to delay their onward journey and spent the night in their carriage for no apparent reason. As part of routine post war checks all baggage was examined and receipts issued for all money carried. Eventually they changed trains at Cologne at the stroke of midnight for Wurzburg where they caught a through train to Munich.

Dalton, left, and friend in front of Cologne Cathedral, August 1922. (Mabel Barker Collection)

After spending time recuperating from their long journey, they set off the next day and began the scenic and dramatic approach to the Alps and Mayrhofen.

On reaching Mayrhofen on Thursday 3rd August the group's luggage was transferred to small carts and pack mules, which then made the eight-mile journey to the camp at Schliffstein, finally arriving in the evening. Amazingly, after such hectic travelling not one of the 30 people or 90 pieces of luggage was missing! Their route followed Rosshag, Breitlahner, Grawand, Alpenrose and Berliner hüttes where rates averaged 1/- for a bed and two

'Brothers Millican and pack mule at the Breitlahner.'
(Mabel Barker Collection)

meals. As a cheaper option the group prepared to base themselves in tents and hired a plot of land for a small ground rent. Due to the lack of flat camping ground their pitch was far from ideal and was sloping and rather exposed. Dalton, the professional camper, was unhappy with the site and wanted to move to an adjacent pitch. However, the owner, who lived in the Berliner hütte, wanted too much money so they decided to stay put. Upon an initial scouting expedition they arranged to take a large party up to the Grawand hütte on the 6th for a couple of nights, which was for most their first experience on a glacier.

Dalton taught the group very patiently the skills of negotiating glaciers, snowfields and the use of ropes and ice axes. His own Alpine skills had been learnt 20 years previously on trips to Switzerland and the like. Further expeditions followed on the 10th August when a party of ten set off for the Greizer hütte. This was a much wilder situation well above the Floitenkees Glacier, surrounded by a ring of jagged black peaks. The party climbed to approximately 9000 feet on the slopes of the Löffler, but for one reason or another did not reach the summit. Interestingly, Mabel's half brother, Pat, also with the group, made friends with a young boy called Franz Knefel. He was from the English Kinderheim in Vienna, who spent a year with George Leigh Mallory at Godalming. At this time Mallory was returning from the first serious, but unsuccessful, attempt to conquer Everest.

Next day, without pause for thought, Dalton led the party on a day outing to the Riffler hütte and two days later on the 13th August Miss Mayer organised a camp festival, during which two young girls performed a short play. The festivities finalised with a campfire, songs and dances. Early the next day Dalton, Miss Hamilton (old friend of Patrick

Dalton, second from right and his group of boys and women. (Mabel Barker Collection)

Taking a breather. Dalton, second from right. (Mabel Barker Collection)

Dalton, second from right, teaching rope techniques. (Mabel Barker Collection)

Crossing snowfields. M. D. second from left. (Mabel Barker Collection)

Geddes) and Gertrude Walmsley (an ex-Saffron Walden student) departed for the Furtschaglhaus. Mabel and a Miss Hirst from Portsmouth met up with them the following morning. It was a clear and sunny day and all had good intentions to cross by the Schoenbichler Horn to the Berliner or Alpenrose hütte in the next valley. Unfortunately, the party drifted off track slightly and ended up on a ridge on which they traversed too far to their left. By now they were lost. Mistakenly, they had climbed a mountain that was not the Schoenbichler Horn but the Talggen Knoff. They continued along the ridge, but then the weather changed for the worse with heavy winds and hail hindering progress, making the consultation of map and compass difficult. In haste the group proceeded downwards along a rough ridge on the other side. For reasons of safety the three novices of the party were roped together, Dalton led the way and Barker was at the rear for most of the time attached to the rope. Time was running out and it was obvious that they may not make it back in daylight. One of the women asked whether they should unrope for speed, to which Barker suggested they should not.

Fortunately Barker's advice proved valuable when a few minutes later a large rock came away in the hands of Gertrude Walmsley and carried her down a steep slope. She was hoisted up alright but had injured her leg. Subsequently, this slowed the party further and as a result darkness fell whilst they were still on the glacier. Finding a sheltered spot amongst the rocks, although soaked and very cold they decided to settle down for the night and proceed in the morning. It then decided to snow, definitely stranding them high above the Alpenrose, at 7000 feet or so. With only half inch of candle in a lantern, food and cigarettes, they huddled together for warmth and spent the long night in good spirits singing and story telling. Luckily for the sporting bunch there was no wind that could have made the situation life threatening. However, a customary violent thunderstorm arrived with most curious and exciting effects. The group sought shelter under a mack-intosh and managed to snuggle together, but on leaving the shelter to rearrange them-selves realised their hair was electrified. Gertrude stood up against the sky and had a halo – every strand of hair had a spark of light on it. More of a cause for concern was the light-ening which struck their ice axes later that night. Regardless of the discomfort, all remained cheery, good tempered and in good spirits. Some managed to grab a little sleep, but all rose as soon as dawn emerged to a wonderful white world and thankfully nobody "woke up dead." Dreaming of their beds and lots of hot coffee, they headed off still in comparative darkness of the shadow of the mountains. On the way down flocks of sheep mobbed the party, Dalton, in no mood for wrangling, thought it necessary to defend himself with his ice axe, which the others thought was a strange spectacle.

Eventually, the party made it to the Alpenrose hütte arriving at 7 am where they were made most welcome. The staff ushered the five of them straight to bed and brought them tea, to which they added spirit without asking. Dalton's reactions, being teetotal, are unclear. However, the kindness of the hütte's occupants was noted. Most of the day was spent asleep in bed, thawing out and regaining energy after their night's exploits. Once recovered they returned back to camp and the rest of the main party later that evening.

Travelling down to the camp in darkness was an experience in itself, as none of them had a lantern. In order to ensure a safe descent Dalton ingeniously tied a white handkerchief around one ankle and held a lit cigarette. Surprisingly nobody was the worse for wear as a result of the unplanned adventure and even Gertrude only had a bruise.

On 18th August Dalton, Barker, Gertrude Walmsley, Dr Thomas (lady) and Miss Venables embarked on an expedition to the Grawand hütte and, with none of them feeling particularly energetic, stayed the night. The next day Dalton returned to the spot where he and the other four had been stranded several days prior, to find and retrieve a climbing rope which had been left on the glacier as it was too stiff and impossible to coil. On returning to the Alpenrose, their accommodation for the night, two of Millican's friends – Wallie and Lottie Camelus – had arrived and wandered up to find them. The group, including the new arrivals, agreed to go over the Schwarzenstein the next day, following a party of English boys and their guide up from the Berliner hütte. Rising early and departing at 5am they sailed up the slopes because none of the climbing was difficult, but according to Barker, Dalton's friend, Lottie, struggled with the steep snow slopes because she was "small and fat!" Ascending over pure white snowfields with a clean atmosphere and cloudless blue sky, they reached the Italian frontier at 11500 feet after six hours. Soldiers had also been up that day marking the frontier with red paint circles on the rocks,

Checking the billycan. (Mabel Barker Collection)

so recently in fact that the paint was still wet! A long time was spent there where Dalton found some waste wood with which he made a fire.

He baked a cake and brewed coffee, whilst all admired the distant views into Italy, Switzerland and away over the Tirol. A descent down the other side to the Greizer hütte in the Fententhal was much steeper with the route heading over a glacier – "poor Lottie had a stiff time!" All arrived back in camp around 8pm, tired, hungry and terribly pleased with themselves. Wallie and Lottie left the party here and set off for Mayrhofen. Around this time Lewis Mumford (native New Yorker internationally recognized as one of the most distinguished urbanists of the 20th Century) and his wife arrived at the camp. Mumford was an ardent admirer of Patrick Geddes and a friend of Gladys Mayer.

With the holiday drawing to a close, Friday 25th was the last opportunity for a serious expedition. Dalton, Franz, Gladys, Reps (a German boy), Mr and Mrs Mumford, Miss Hamilton and Barker went up to the Grawand hütte where they said farewell. The planned trek over the Schumlidiholm the following day was thwarted due to severe thick mist, so rather than miss out, another night was spent at the Alpenrose. Continued misty weather the next morning restricted the group's activities, so the afternoon was spent playing on the Horn Kees, the glacier adjacent to the Berliner hütte. Mr and Mrs Mumford, ill equipped for climbing, did not last long. In the glorious weather of the following day the Mumfords returned to Schliffstein and onto Mayrhofen. The rest of the group tramped over the Schoenbichler Horn, with the path passing directly over the summit. This time they managed to stay on the right track without getting lost and spending another night on the glacier. On the top, Millican found wood, lit a fire, made coffee and tea and dispersed it between the group and various other tourists lucky enough to be on the summit at the same time. All members of the party signed their names in a book that had been left on the top and then descended to the Furtschagelhaus.

'The ruling passion' – Dalton makes tea.
(Mabel Barker Collection)

Relaxing and taking in the sights around camp concluded their stay in the Tirol. Eventually winding up camp at Schliffstein on 30th August, the party then set off on the weary 15-hour 2/- journey from Mayrhofen to Vienna. Seated in second class was uncomfortable and to top it all they spent the night in the corridor, which was fortunately fitted with seats and wide-open windows. To finalise the holiday a small number of the group crossed the Brenner into Italy for a look at the Dolomites. Barker and Miss Hamilton stayed in Wien for three days but Dalton decided to precede them to Cortina. Dalton and Barker, the only remaining climbers, continued to sample the climbing and according to Mabel "had a small taste of the lovely quality of rock." At the end of the venture Dalton was very tired – not that surprising at 55 years old. All remaining members of the party returned to England at Tre Croce, except for Dalton who went his own way to meet a friend.

14
High Heavens Camp.

Stitching a tent at High Heavens Camp, March 1933.

Towards the end of the roaring 1920s a Mr C. J. Brake advertised some of his leafy Buckinghamshire estate for sale in the London evening newspapers. The land was in the secluded valley of Marlow Bottom situated in the Chiltern Hills and was one of Buckinghamshire's wildest spots, where plots costing up to £50 could be obtained.

Several families, looking for a better way of life in the countryside, moved to the valley from the 'big smoke.' In complete contrast to the city, the valley was a heavily wooded, fertile sea of green and was spacious, peaceful, clean and safe. At first, holiday homes and weekend getaways made-up the majority of dwellings, but some folk lived there full-time. The majority of residents made their homes from wooden huts, corrugated iron shacks and tents, resulting in the area becoming known as 'Tin Town' or 'Shanty Town.' Apparently, all those who lived in Marlow Bottom appeared to be of a strange character, leading people to unfairly assume that the district was full of gypsies and gruesome characters. To others it had become known as an area of intellectual dropouts.

Dalton, wishing to be closer to his brother Henry who had married and moved to nearby Jordans in 1922, also acquired a plot of land around 1929, presumably with money from Walnut Cottage. It is generally assumed that the Professor of Adventure never lived under a roof again after quitting work, but in reality it was only when he left Walnut Cottage that he actually gave up his bricks and mortar home.

Interestingly, excerpts from literature available from Mr Brake's estate, which Dalton no doubt read, stated:

***Particulars of Cheap Freehold Land for Sale on The Marlow Estate**. The prettiest part of Buckinghamshire, only 28 miles from London, 19 miles from Uxbridge, 25 miles from Ealing and 27 miles from Acton. The County of Buckinghamshire is considered by those of authority to be unrivalled for its many beauty spots, amongst which the Marlow District stands pre-eminent, whilst its climate is unequalled, being particularly noted for its bracing character and tonic-like effect. Prospective clients should not miss this unique* *opportunity of securing some really excellent land in this pretty and most healthy neighbourhood, so readily accessible to London and its suburbs and entirely unspoilt.*

Was this tonic-like effect a contributing factor behind his move and had Loughton become polluted? Adding to the attraction of the area was the fact that:

Sportsmen *have plenty of scope: good boating, fishing and bathing can be enjoyed to the usual sports. Numerous rambles through shady lanes and footpaths and beautiful woods may be enjoyed without being isolated. Conveniently, the Estate is situate adjoining the Town of Marlow in the Rural District (thus escaping Urban Rates) and is within ten minutes walk of the Station and River and occupies a truly delightful position high up on the spur of the Chiltern Hills, thus enjoying views of the Quarry Woods and overlooking the Thames Valley. By reason of its altitude the land is perfectly dry. Thus the land especially appeals to the City Worker and others requiring rest and quietude away from the hustle and bustle of the Metropolis.*

Ironically, although produced as a circular, these particulars almost seem to have been directly aimed at Dalton, the ex-city worker who had been searching for a quiet place to live for the past 30 years. At this point a definite pattern becomes apparent; as one area became overpopulated he liberated himself and relocated to another more peaceful location. Evidently, he purchased one of the more affordable plots away from the busy Main Wycombe Road. The particulars specified them as:

Cheap plots – *other choice plots having frontages to pretty secluded roads are for sale from £10 each upwards. The majority are 20 feet by 200 feet and at this absurdly low figure represent more than value for money.*

His land was a long strip from the edge of High Heavens Wood which ran down to High Heavens Lane, on which he first lived in an improvised tent close up against the woods in a sort of bohemian camp. This was to become known as High Heavens Camp for obvious reasons.

He lived alone, but many people had homes close by and was not isolated in any way. Amongst the scanty population was a collection of differing people. Mr and Mrs Hockin, his nearest neighbours, lived in the luxury of a small brick and flint bungalow. Doctor Durrant owned a large sanatorium at White Hill and Mr Lane, owner of a little wooden shop on the edge of Munces Wood, sold food and paraffin. He also acted as milkman. Other provisions could be obtained from baker, 'Billy Hunter', who sold fresh bread from his pony and trap. Further to the inhabitants was a queer nattering woman called Miss Poole, who seemed something of an invalid. She was also unconventional and similar to Dalton in certain ways. Helen M. Poole, her full name but better known as Pixie Poole, was Irish from a titled background.

Pixie resided in a caravan on her own, she too had opted out of society and chose to live a solitary existence on her own means. On her land she grew vegetables, kept a goat and lived no more than 30 yards away from where Millican had his patch, living on the opposite side to the Hockins. Cycling was also her mode of transport.

Even though they led similar lifestyles they tended to have nothing to do with each other, but this was more through Dalton's choice than hers. Pixie chased him everywhere and had fallen in love years before. As time passed she became increasingly irritable and would often creep about insulting folk. It was well known that the two of them had the most dreadful rows. On one particular occasion Pixie was seen running around in her nightdress in the early hours yelling that Dalton had been in her caravan. Supposedly, nothing came of the accusation. Had he been in her caravan or not and if so what was he doing? As one of her closest neighbours he may well have just been a scapegoat?

'Old Dalton,' as many knew him, was frequently seen pushing, sometimes riding, his famous old blue bike – rumoured to be a woman's bike – along the Valley and also on his infrequent trips through Badgebury Woods and down Oaktree Road to Marlow where he would travel for supplies. More often than not he was seen to walk much more than

'Mr Dalton climbing a large tree near his camp', 1933. (Sunday Chronicle)

he cycled. Additional to his excursions to Marlow were trips to nearby High Wycombe where he would visit the library or meet up with family for tea and coffee. Contact was maintained with family and he frequently visited Henry and wife 'Goldie' in Jordans, which was within a short distance. Often, if not cycling, he would walk across the fields from Seer Green village. Henry and 'Goldie' had met on a Professor of Adventure camping holiday to Loch Lomond and lived with their children Nicholas and Nancy. Occasionally, when Millican was a little short of money, Henry would slip him a £5 note on the understanding that he need not repay it. This was to the amazement of Millican's nephew, Nick, whose weekly pocket money was only one penny! Although more than welcome, he never stayed more than a night or so as he could not bear a roof over his head for long. During visits to Jordans he would scope the village wood, which contained plenty of holly trees – an abundant source of tent pegs!

Pottering around High Heavens Camp or the valley, developing his plans for further thrills, working on his programme, contemplating new theories on life, creation, the world in general and searching for answers formed much of his day. Growing older and slightly reserved he became less famed for his free and comprehensive outdoor instruction to local townsfolk. Generally he tended not to mix with other locals all that much and rarely went out of his way to speak to other people, though he would often pass the time of day with anybody he chanced to meet on the road. However, when he returned from guiding on the continent the children in the valley acted as a keen audience. Gathering anxiously at Dalton's camp, they sat, silent and wide eyed, listening intently to his stories of adventures in wonderful far away places. Photographs shuffled around the audience adding to the excitement. Gasps and ahs intensified as the stories progressed. Foreign travel was still relatively uncommon and to many made Millican something of a maverick. Of particular amusement to the children were his puttees, which always left his knobbly knees bare. Meanwhile, Henry Dalton was providing his own entertainment for local villagers in nearby Jordans. On returning from family holidays, such as visits to Corsica, he would organise magic lantern shows in the village hall.

Millican was very much liked by the locals and it was of the general opinion that he was a delightfully interesting man, with nothing frightening or untoward about him. They thought he spoke beautifully, was honest, well educated and a real gentleman who never bothered anybody and kept himself to himself. It was obvious that he came from a good family and all respected him, even though some thought he was somewhat of a hermit in a pleasant way. Valley residents rarely knew where he would be, as he would come and go. During fine weather though, he would often be seen seated on a bank at the side of the road, his bike propped up, enjoying a smoke and reading a newspaper. Quitting work was an achievement the Professor of Adventure was proud of and on many occasions told his neighbours "I used to work in the City but felt stifled."

In future years, Dalton was to build a hut for himself for use in the colder months and forfeit the tent for something a little more comfortable. The wooden hut, free from all extravagance, was similar to the Epping hut and again housed a fire. In the centre of the hut was a metal grate on which he burnt large logs, smoke escaped through an opening in the roof directly above the grate. On some occasions logs, over six feet in length, protruded outside the hut. Each log was carefully nurtured, rotated, kicked now and again and produced terrific heat. They always burnt to dust. Visitors left in disbelief with his seemingly unconcerned burning of timber in a highly flammable wooden hut!

Millican Dalton became a more than common sight wandering the outstanding natural beauty of the Chiltern Hills. Much enjoyment was had travelling through the abundant beech woods, quaint villages and down the leafy lanes, rucksack over shoulder and cigarette in hand.

15
The 'Cave Hotel.'

The view towards the Jaws of Borrowdale from within the 'Cave Hotel.' M. D. silhouetted amongst the trees c. 1940.

Camping at High Lodore was considered the perfect spot, but life under canvas was only really a temporary measure due to the wet Cumberland weather and so a search for other more permanent possibilities began. During the start of the 20th century, Millican, along with some of his adventurous friends, began exploring caves, most formed by the slate quarrying process.

These man-made caves provided a lightweight alternative to camping in tents, as less gear could be carried and was a further progression from his early gear experiments. Benefits of easy access to the fells and rock and the best possible shelter from the elements was provided. One such cave, at Rydal near Grasmere on the slopes of Loughrigg, a vast, dank and sludgy cavern, witnessed overnight stays, but due to its unsuitability was discounted.

From at least 1914 another option, a disused split level quarried cave proved ideal and was adopted as his residence during the summer months. A more scenic location could not have been chosen. It was amongst outstanding beauty situated deep in the mesmerising Jaws of Borrowdale. A romantic land blanketed with oak and birch woodland, divided by the emerald glide of the crystal clear River Derwent, possibly the most scenic square mile in the whole of Lakeland. The cave, situated directly under Castle Crag on its easterly flank, acted as the perfect base from which to operate. No compromise was made on his choice of 'home' with the lower cave extending

Castle Crag seen from Bowderstone Pinnacle.

ninety feet into the crag, covering an approximate area of four thousand five hundred feet square. The upper level, interlinked with the lower and just under half the size, was referred to by Dalton as the 'Attic.' It was here where he had his living area. Inside was dark and damp, but ample dry areas existed with excellent shelter provided from the wind and rain, due to the topography around the entrance.

Subsequently, he claimed the cave as his own, and jokingly renamed it the 'Cave Hotel' and 'Aladdin's Cave.' Inside was equipped with 'artefacts' recovered from Grange tip. An abundance of gadgets and wires suspended cookware on and around his fire, shelves provided storage for books and newspapers. Quarried debris covered the floor, some of which had been used to construct dry stone walls and seating with an adjacent fireplace. A fire, which was burnt almost constantly kept the cave warm, provided light and was hot enough to cook anything. Through years of practice he became a campfire expert. Knowing that larch, juniper, yew and holly burnt the best and longest, his fires were efficient and effective. Ample supplies of timber could be found outside the cave in High Hows Wood. Firewood was cut with a bowsaw and there was always a plentiful supply, stacked and ready to burn.

Water, constantly flowing through a fissure in the ceiling, provided a year-round supply and was the only thing that broke the silence of the subdued ambience. Barrels, again from Grange tip, caught the dripping water which was used for drinking, cooking and on rare occasions washing. Terraces outside the cave, formed by mining operations, also it seems had a use and witnessed the cultivation of potatoes.

There is no doubt that the 'Cave Hotel' was considered an unpleasant place by most, but in reality, was relative luxury compared to life in a tent. Even friends and family agreed after spending a night in the 'Attic.' Evidence of his existence exists in the 'Attic' in the form of a carved inscription at its entrance stating bluntly: 'Don't!! waste worrds, jump to conclusions!' This particular carving, one of several in and around the cave, is the basis of much discussion. It is rumoured in some circles that the carvings are not those of Millican Dalton but those of a friend. Apparently, during a raging argument with a Scottish friend, the Scot went to his car and returned with a hammer, chisel and punch and carved the motto in exasperation with Millican protesting in horror alongside. Millican tried to stifle the arguments and often told his friend "Don't jump to conclusions!" The Scot was so irritated that he hastily carved with a hammer and punch rather than a chisel. Careful analysis of the carving does in fact give the impression that a punch was used. However, curiously the inscription is signed M.D. The incorrect spelling of words, apparently a joke between the two friends, is possibly an expression of a rolling 'R'. Another inscription, 'F. M. A GOOD COMRADE RMD 1935,' adorns the entrance to the lower cave and looks very much like Dalton's writing.

The approach to the 'Cave Hotel.'

Friends knew when the Professor of Adventure was in residence by the blue-grey plume of smoke that emanated from the cave entrance up the face of Castle Crag. Most visitors to the cave remember the difficulty in finding it, over rock, through trees and up scree. Whilst escorting guests, attention would be drawn to the way Mother Nature tried to camouflage the spoil heaps around the caves. Ralph H. Mayson considered the approach to the cave from Rosthwaite to be a "delightful journey, particularly in the month of June, when the wild roses are gracing the edges in the lane to the bridge over the River Derwent and, turning to the right and following the river bank, he (Dalton) would pause to admire the yellow iris in the swamps, and the buck bean rising from the small dark bog holes."

Access to the cave could be gained from either Grange to the north, along the track to Hollows Farm and then parallel to the banks of the River Derwent or from the south via Rosthwaite. Alternatively, a shorter, more adventurous but colder route could be gained by fording the river. Those who cared to drop by enjoyed fire, coffee and stimulating conversation. Stories around his magical campfires were many and formed the basis of a good evening. Apart from the usual banter regarding climbing and current affairs, Dalton also discussed his theories and as he grew older tried to lure friends into light-hearted arguments, although he tended to be hard to argue with and became increasingly stubborn. Those who knew him were well aware of his opinionated personality and rarely took him on. "In this cave he would entertain his visitors empounding to them the philosophy which was purely Millican Dalton," added Mayson. Scary ghost stories, for which he was noted, provided yet more entertainment. Waiting till after dark he would sit his audience around the fire, dish out hot drinks and with his most excellent and diverse imagination proceed in scaring their wits out. On many occasions visitors would be so encapsulated in the evening's events that darkness would fall without them realising. Making the point, Mabel M. Barker wrote "The charm of his camp fire and coffee and his (increasingly argumentative!) conversation delayed departure till the dusk caught us."

Sometimes guests would be invited to ascend the north side of Castle Crag, an interestingly steep scramble over rough steep ground, rock, and grass and through clinging trees. Once on the summit a full and rewarding panorama greeted all successful initiates. Accurately describing the views Mayson continued: "Here Millican would point out, to the North, Derwentwater and Skiddaw with the village of Grange and the River Derwent in the foreground; to the East, Grange Fell or King's How as it is now called, with Helvellyn in the far distance; to the South the head of Borrowdale Valley, with Rosthwaite village, above which Ullscarf stands out on the skyline. The stream descending Greenup Ghyll can faintly be seen with Eagle Crag on the right, which marks the junction of the two streams, Greenup and Langstrath. Rosthwaite Fell and Coombe Ghyll come next in turn, overshadowed by Glaramara, then Great End, Scafell, Base Brown and Great Gable, with Grains Ghyll and Sty Head Pass leading out from the hamlet of Seathwaite; to the West, Gate Crag with its wonderful scrambling gullies and short rock climbs and the lovely stream which comes down between Gate Crag and Knitting Howe; in between and down below, runs the track between Grange and Seatoller. All these places were familiar to Millican."

Many people simply visited the cave whilst they had chance before he left for the continent or made his return south. An entry in the F.& R.C.C. Borrowdale climbing book on the 9th August 1914, days after England's declaration of war against Germany, was written by W. Allsop, an occasional climbing partner. He stated that whilst at a F.& R.C.C. Meet in Buttermere he ventured over Honister Pass to Dalton's camp at Castle Crag. Later he meandered down to Lodore before returning to rejoin the rest of the group in Buttermere. A visitor's book within the cave even encouraged guests to leave their mark.

Another visitor to the 'Cave Hotel' was Charles Rolland, he said: "I got to know him in 1936 or '37 or both. We used to have family holidays at Rosthwaite, staying in Rose Cottage which was attached to the village Post Office and Store and was run by Ernie and Grace Plaskett. Millican was living in the cave on Castle Crag and he used to come down to Rosthwaite to mend his boots in Ernie's workshop. There I met him and we used to have long conversations about climbing. I was very keen but had little experience. He told me about Doves' Nest Caves in Combe Ghyll on Glaramara. He fired my enthusiasm and I set off to explore them and the rocks around them. He did not offer to come with me. I would go by myself complete with candles for the darker recesses.

In the evenings I would find my way through the woods to the cave, equipped with a paper packet of Woodbine cigarettes, two pence in those days. They would keep Millican happy and he would talk to me for an hour or two and ply me with coffee. The cave was very well suited to his needs. Over the fire he had an iron bar from which hung an assortment of cans on hooks made from fencing wire. He did not bother about washing up – there was a special can for each thing he wanted to heat, tea, coffee, soup, porridge and so on. The spoil heap below the cave supplied plenty of slates, which served as plates. They went out in the rain as necessary.

I did not see him afloat on his raft, "Rogue Herries." My recollection is that he had a bike, which he hid in the bracken beside the track to Grange. He used to go to Keswick on the bike and when he was migrating south the old bike almost vanished under the collection of goods which he hung from it.

There was a large photo of him, complete with felt hat and pheasant's feather in the glass doorway of Birkett's boot shop in St John's Street.

Ernie Plaskett used to show off to visitors. He once asked two ladies if they had seen "The oldest living thing in the valley" meaning the Borrowdale Yews at Seathwaite. He was much amused when they replied "Oh yes, you mean the Cave Man." Millican did not think that was funny."

Amongst other daily rituals was the morning walk to the Post Office in Grange-in-Borrowdale. Not only did this jaunt allow him to collect his post and a copy of his favourite newspaper, the *Daily Herald*, it was also an opportunity to catch up on conversation. Political preferences, views and leanings are clearly reflected in his choice of daily newspaper. The leftwing *Daily Herald* commonly portrayed capitalists as devils, never condemned strikers and, unlike other newspapers, took an anti-war stance at the outbreak of the Great War. Importantly the fact that Dalton actually bought a newspaper demonstrates a tie with society and a wish to remain informed of current affairs – not the actions of a true hermit.

Castle Crag sparkles with many interesting features, but it was the south side that Dalton particularly loved. The Scotch Firs, High Doat, the ancient deciduous woodland of Johnny Wood and Charity Coppice with its secret waterfall hidden away from the crowds were favourite spots and only a short distance from camp. Irrespective to the permanency of the 'Cave Hotel' he would not hesitate at throwing up a tent or bivouac whenever the need arose. A large rock, directly facing the lower Seathwaite Slabs, provided the best natural shelter in the vicinity and was often used for an overnight stop after Fell and Rock Meets or when on the alternative route to the crags around Great Gable. Stan Edmundson from Seathwaite recalls Dalton sleeping under the rock. "Millican Dalton would come to Seathwaite and sit in our garden, have a pot of tea, scones and cake," said Stan. "He would sleep under a large rock at Seathwaite Slabs. He always wore shorts, army type jacket; never wore socks, just bandages around his feet. Millican got about on a bike for which he made a carrier from hazel branches bound by string. Millican was a wonderful character when Borrowdale was a quiet, beautiful valley."

Dalton's overnight shelter at Seathwaite Slabs.

Dalton's right to camp long-term on land obviously owned by somebody else is of some interest. Did he ever seek permission from the landowner? No records detailing a concession between the two parties appears to exist. Up until 1919 Castle Crag was privately owned, but was donated to the National Trust in 1920 by Sir William Hamer and his family in memory of his son John and the men of Borrowdale who fell in the First World War – they possibly turned a blind eye to his activities. Subsequently, a further bequest to the National Trust was made in 1939, when Lady Hamer gave 18.6 hectares on the lower slopes of Castle Crag, along with its resident 'caveman' and 'Cave Hotel,' as a memorial to Sir William Hamer. In the early days of the National Trust the enforcement of camping byelaws was not an issue. Wild camping was rela-

tively uncommon and not seen in a bad light. It seems that as Dalton was the only camper in the caves and as he caused no destruction or nuisance, he was left alone unhindered. Whatever the agreement between Dalton, the Hamers and the National Trust, if any, on returning from the south his 'Aladdin's Cave' would be found intact, undisturbed and uninhabited with all his 'possessions' ready and available for immediate use.

As would be expected, Dalton owned very little. One of his few possessions, probably his most prized, was his sewing machine, which meant the manufacture and maintenance of clothing and equipment was not restricted solely to his southern residences. Although technology was progressing at a rapid rate, the 'Cave Hotel' was not left completely behind and the addition of the sewing machine ensured some degree of modernism.

The lower cave. Millican cooking under a tepee frame – note the sewing machine, 3rd September 1919. (Mabel Barker Collection)

16
Rogue Herries and Millican Dalton.

Afloat on 'Rogue Herries' c. 1930. (Mayson Collection)

Many people for their own personal reasons are drawn to the Lake District and it was Keswick's attractions that lured Hugh Walpole, the New Zealand born author, to buy Brackenburn at Manesty above Derwentwater in 1923. Several family holidays to the region as a child had developed a longing to return. The purchase of his "little paradise on Catbells" subsequently provided a retreat from his hectic literary lifestyle that saw him in much demand, travelling feverishly between London and the USA to attend various functions. Upon arrival in Keswick he was keen to be involved in all aspects of day-to-day life and soon became a respected figure of the community. Despite staying at his escape in the Lakes for generally no longer than a fortnight, his visits and accompanied social interaction at local events still enabled him to become acquainted with most colourful personalities of the area, including Millican Dalton.

On Christmas Eve 1927 Walpole commenced writing his family saga novels, the Herries Chronicles. *Rogue Herries*, the first of the novels, was first published in 1930. This splendid work of fiction, depicted in eighteenth century Cumberland, is a fine, adventurous and wonderful story of a split family set amidst throngs of strange characters, romance, murder, weddings and feuds. Walpole had an excellent geographical knowledge of the county, which became more than apparent in his works. Locations, panoramas and famous landmarks abound which give the reader an authentic sense of reality. Taking the leading role in the story is Francis 'Rogue' Herries, known as the Dark Angel of Borrowdale.

Typically, the source of inspiration for many authors is a result of real life encounters. Indeed Walpole's familiarity with Millican provided him with a ready-made character. Dalton looked as if he had been in a time gap with a similar appearance to that of an eighteenth century vagrant and therefore resulted in his astonishing inclusion in *Rogue Herries*.

Rogue Herries:
Part Two *'Forty-five –* Into the Cave

[About Herries] *He woke to a strange sense of constriction. He moved and found amazingly that his arms and legs were tied with rough rope. He raised his head and stared into the eyes of a man who sat motionless on a rock near him.*

[About the man] *He was a man with a thin dry face, long shaggy black hair, a coat and breeches of some colour that had faded into a dirty green. He looked like part of the fell. His legs were thin and long and sharp. He was not young, fifty years of age maybe...The man was, from his voice, not of the North. His tone was firm, quiet, reflective...He was of great height and very thin with a long nose.*

[About Herries] *He saw then the grey opening of a cave in the hill, fenced with dead bracken and furze. At first he could see nothing, but could smell cooking food, an odd sweet scent of flowers and a musty animal tang. The man had his hand on his arm and very gently, as though he were speaking to a child, said: "Sit you there. You can sleep if you will. The straw's dry." Francis turned back, shifting the bracken a little and the sun flickered on to him, dancing before his eyes...He sat up and looked about him. The sun streamed in from the fell. He could see all the cave, which was not indeed quite a cave, but rather the opening of some deserted entrance to a long-neglected mine. In the black cavern beyond him there was a fire and on the fire a round black pot.*

Comparisons between Walpole's 'fictitious' character and the Professor of Adventure are astounding and seem to be more than coincidence. Obviously Dalton did not bind folk but he was renowned for routinely carrying an Alpine rope. His black, grey streaked hair was longer than the usual, fashionable 'short back and sides' of the day; it *was* shaggy and never appeared to be combed. Describing his outward appearance identically Mabel M. Barker said his clothing was of "...a dull green, toning with the fells." His legs *were* actually thin and long and sharp. In addition, by the time Walpole penned the first words of *Rogue Herries*, Dalton was *not* young. He was sixty years old, sufficiently close to the estimated fifty years of age. Although having lived in Cumberland for the first thirteen years of his life, when Walpole arrived in Keswick Dalton had spent the previous forty-three years living in the South and had lost his northern accent, giving the impression he was not from the locality. He *was* tall and thin – in excess of six foot tall and of a lean physique. Interestingly, access to the 'Cave Hotel' is gained by a walkway, which in summer becomes encircled with towering fronds of bracken and nettles. Bracken, taken into the cave, formed the basis of his sleeping arrangements. Finally and probably the most defining resemblance is the fact that the 'Cave Hotel' is not a cave as such, but the remnant of a long terminated stone quarrying process.

Furthermore to Walpole's composition, it is well known that the 'Skipper' constructed many rafts. Significantly, the best known of all must be the one he proudly christened 'Rogue Herries.' On first impressions this craft would not inspire any confidence or assurance of safety to any modern-day sailing instructor or seadog, but undoubtedly worked, as he used it to sail down the River Derwent and across Derwentwater. Constructed from a combination of tree branches, several empty barrels recovered from Grange tip provided buoyancy and were all bound together to form his vessel. It was steered by the provision of a tiller, mast and a red junk-style sail and finished off with a hand written name plaque on the bow. The naming of this raft is again, more than coincidence. Of course, he enjoyed the tale, it made excellent reading and encapsulated loved and frequented locations. It was in the right style, but ultimately the naming was not merely a sign of appreciation of compelling literature, but a discreet acknowledgement to Walpole of his inclusion in a classic that was recognised on an international stage.

Photographic artist Ralph H. Mayson ensured that this acknowledgement was captured on film and the photograph of Dalton sat astride his raft, at a point on the River Derwent known as Gowd Dub, has probably become the most recognisable image of all. Whether or not the photograph was stage-managed, a definite play was made to the camera. Close to the riverbank in what looks to be an unnavigable depth of water, conveniently the lettering on the name plaque was large and faced directly towards the photographer. Published as another publicity postcard by Mayson and available from his Emporium, the card was sold, with its underlying significance, to unsuspecting tourists.

Descriptions, similarities and acknowledgements of this nature are not simply a twist of fate and without doubt Dalton was immortalised as Hugh Walpole's character – George Endicott.

17

Elementary my dear Watson.

THE CREVICE. SLINGSBY'S CHIMNEY, SCAFELL. 420.

Dalton, (centre) climbing with friends on Slingsby's Chimney. (Mayson Collection)

Further to a progressive influx of tourists into the Lake District after the turn of the 19th century, guiding businesses took advantage of the increased numbers of people wishing to enter the fells. These tourists were, in general, far less daunted than the early Victorians and much keener to experience the 'savageness' of the mountains. No longer were mountains purely the domain of shepherds, gentleman explorers or pioneers, they had become available to all.

J. E. B. Wright established one such business, The Lakeland Mountain Guides, in 1925. Jerry Wright, known as the 'Keswick Guide,' based his business at Seatoller House, Borrowdale, near the foot of Honister Pass. Guiding was primarily for groups or individuals who wished to hike, but he also catered for those wanting to experience rock climbing.

In 1927 the Journal of the F.& R.C.C. contained an article in the Editor's Notes relating to a pamphlet titled *The Fell Guide to the English Lakes*, which it branded as "American advertising and the cheap press, that is perhaps only to be expected in our modern age." High pricing and the strong advertising medium was highly frowned upon which according to the Journal, "Makes rock-climbing a sport for plutocrats, instead of what it essentially is, the most democratic of all recreations." The pamphlet, produced by Wright, was his idea of a forward thinking approach to advertising in order to attract increased custom, listing plainly and simply available routes and tariffs. Fees seemed rather high with guiding services priced at five guineas per day for each guide for specific courses as selected by Mr Wright on Pillar Rock. Wright's attitude towards the F.& R.C.C. article was one of contempt and to show his skill and ability scaled Napes Needle in sixty-five seconds – a more than impressive feat. Needless to say Wright made several enemies.

In direct competition was The British Mountain Guides, established in 1933, under the direction of Stanley Watson and based at Grosvenor House, Blencathra Street, Keswick. Prior to the formation of the British Mountain Guides, Wright employed Watson as a guide. Adopting a similar advertising format to the Lakeland Mountain Guides, Watson placed posters around the area, in particular Newton Place opposite the Borrowdale Hotel and charged up to £1 a day per person for a typical ascent of Napes Needle and up to five other equally difficult climbs, dependant upon conditions of the rock and ability of the climber.

A resulting dispute with Watson left Wright considering legal action against alleged libellous statements in a B.M.G. poster that ambiguously referred to Wright and his business. Advised accordingly, Wright chose not to pursue the action.

Occasionally, Watson employed Dalton during the mid-thirties to guide clients when overburdened with work. For this he received 15s a day to guide on popular routes such as those on Great Gable or on Pillar Rock, as advertised on posters of the B.M.G. No other person could have been more suitable than Dalton who was a steadfast old hand. Although employed in his late sixties he was obviously regarded by Watson as a competent and prudent leader, more than capable of the job role.

Except for occasionally relieving the B. M. G. his own programme remained full with the period between the two world wars the best trade. Clearly the Professor of Adventure competed with both the B. M. G. and the L. M. G. but as custom was high there was sufficient trade for all concerned. Dalton had built an extensive client base, many of who returned year after year. As far as can be gathered, Dalton never received any bad press for his guiding or advertising and cared little about Wright's and Watson's quibbles.

Considering that Dalton's advertising medium was just as strong as Wright's and actually preceded it by at least 12 years, it is of interest that he was never condemned or challenged by the F.& R.C.C. as they did with Wright's pamphlet. What seemed to have passed unnoticed within the depths of the F.& R.C.C. is the fact that Dalton's article, *A Camping Holiday*, was nothing more than a blatant advertising stunt. This article is a clear adaptation of his programme from the previous year and, as a result, he managed to manipulate the Journal into a free advertising medium. Without question Millican Dalton was something of a self-publicist.

18
The Caveman 1941.

The Caveman,
1941

MODEL C
IN
BRI

The "Cave Hotel" Mr. D
calls his residence. Here
The cooking utensils have
salvaged from scrap dumps,
holding the cigarette in
toes to keep the ash from
into his porridge.

PLUCKY BRI
TO WEAR R

★ Mr. Millican Dalton, the ★
Old Man of the Cave...
Tyrolean hat with
heron's feather, plaid
over a brown coat and
even the icicles can't
stop him wearing
shorts.

ITALY GIVES US ONE WEEK

Dalton achieved nationwide publicity when he appeared on page 7 of the Daily Mirror in January 1941.
(Daily Mirror)

Not even snow, ice and sub-zero temperatures could prevent Dalton's occupancy of the 'Cave Hotel' over the winter of 1940/41. World War Two was well underway and although the evacuation of thousands of children to the Buckinghamshire countryside was considered to be a safe option, its close proximity to London presented too much of a threat to Dalton. Unlike his determination throughout the Great War to carry on with normal life, the increased risks posed by the heavy aerial bombardment of the Luftwaffe and the high possibility of invasion resulted in his own evacuation to Borrowdale. As a matter of fact the 'Cave Hotel' was probably the best air-raid shelter in England and provided an ideal retreat from the Blitz devastation in and around the capital.

Keswick residents, familiar only with his summer visits, became aware of his uncharacteristic out-of-season residency down the valley. This caught the imagination of many and was soon picked up on by the media. It was evident that Dalton did not shy away from press coverage, on the contrary and in fact was the subject of many newspaper articles in which he seemed to actually enjoy relaying his story, although maintaining his modesty. However, no matter how unpretentious the Professor of Adventure was, he could not escape some greater amount of publicity after featuring in an article in the national tabloid newspaper, the *Daily Mirror*, on January 21st 1941, whose circulation figures had reached 1.7 million. The article, titled 'The Caveman 1941,' written by a special correspondent, described how war could not touch him.

"Millican Dalton threw up his job to live among the hills of the Lake District. He didn't look for a country cottage overlooking a lake. He chose, at Borrowdale, a cave as high as a three-storey house set in the wooded crags above the river. Today this seventy-three year old hermit is less affected by the war than any man in Britain. Peep into Millican's home. He wears a Tyrolese hat decorated with a heron's feather, a plaid over a brown coat, green corduroy shorts, puttees and climbing boots. He makes tents, builds rafts and is a Lake District guide," read the article.

Rationing posed few problems mainly due to his simple living and ability to reap wild food and manufacture his own clothing. He told the correspondent "My only luxury is coffee, for which I pay 2s. 2d. per lb. I sleep on a bed of bracken and need only my plaid and an eiderdown to keep me warm. I don't burn a light, though I lie in bed from beginning to end of blackout." Unlike other civilians living conventional lives it was clear Dalton cared nothing for the blackout. After failing in an attempt to contain the light within the confines of the cave, he sacrificed the obligatory campfire and refrained from burning candles.

However, his decision to remain in darkness was not through his own choice and only made after a visit to the cave in 1940 by the Air Raid Warden for Keswick who told him that he must not show a light. This infuriated Millican and incited him to write several letters to 10 Downing Street. They detailed his disapproval for government policies and urged Prime Minister, Winston Churchill, to call an immediate end to the battling as it was interfering with his liberty! Yet, despite Millican's efforts, Churchill ignored the pleas and rightly or wrongly continued with the allied offensive. Apparently he never received a reply.

"Seven hours sleep is enough for anyone. The rest of the time I just lie and think and listen," said the Professor of Adventure who had become one with his surroundings, not just in appearance, but also with his affection for all things wild, claiming "You can't feel lonely with nature as your companion." If that was not enough to keep him entertained there was always the pitter-patter of water dripping from the ceiling of the cave and the crashing of icicles from the crags above the cave entrance.

Accompanying his expenditure on coffee was food and tobacco that came out of his weekly allowance of 22s. His weekly income is well worth analysing. Through a study by the Ministry of Labour, of which figures became public on 14th January 1941, it was ascertained that the average man in the street was spending 10s 10d per week on rent and 6s 5d on lighting and fuel. In comparison, Dalton must have been reasonably comfortable on his 22s considering his minimal living expenses.

Two photographs featured in the article and clearly showed the man – he looked an amazing figure. The main photograph, taking up nearly a full page, pictured Dalton outside the lower portion of the cave against a curtain, almost a portcullis, of impressive six-foot long icicles. Not forgetting the great man was now aged 73; he was still wearing shorts while all others in Borrowdale sat cuddled up in front of their raging coal fires. In the second smaller photograph he was captured stirring his pan of porridge with a burning cigarette held between his toes in an attempt to prevent ash from falling into his breakfast – proof if ever it was needed that he was a chain smoker.

The *Whitehaven News* then printed their own article on 30th January 1941, with the headline 'Borrowdale's caveman cooking a meal.' The article read:

Meet Mr Millican Dalton. He is one of the creatures of the wild. He lives in a cave high up in one of the wooded crags that are the glory of Borrowdale. In the photograph he is stirring the porridge he is making, taking care to put the cigarette he is smoking between a big toe and a smaller toe that the tobacco ash may not drop into the breakfast. Mr Dalton is 73½ years of age, is tall, spare, hard as a fell toad and if you were to meet him you would agree that in his Tyrolese hat, decorated by a heron's plume, his plaid drawn over a brown tweed coat, his green corduroy shorts, sinewy legs, sometimes encased in puttees and climbing boots, he looks a fine figure of a man.

We last met him 20 years ago at the foot of Taylor's Gill Force in Seathwaite. Then, as on this day, he was stirring porridge in precisely the same fashion. He was conducting a climbing party on the Napes Ridge and, joining us, did a Kern Knott climb, the Napes Needle and the Arrowhead Arête. One experience that day is unforgettable. Mr Dalton had with him a man who lost his nerve and would neither go forward nor backward and in the pitch in which he lay stuck we had to climb over his body, leaving his guide to extricate him as best he could. We asked Mr Dalton if he remembered the incident and after a while, for 20 years is a long time, the memory of it came back to him.

It was on the coldest and bitterest day of this year that we renewed our acquaintance with this man of the wilds. The icicles hung like a curtain across the mouth of a cave high as a three-storied house and roomy enough to hold one or two companies of soldiers. Water, which seeps through the roof of the cave, was also icicles and divided it into two. Millican Dalton's part of it is only a few yards square. It is walled in by slate offal. Everything within is "wondrous neat and clean." Cleverly packed is the cave-dweller's camp equipment and the cooking utensils, which have all been picked out of village dumps. There was a place for everything and everything was in its place. In one corner was Millican Dalton's lying-up place. Bracken for a bed and a plaid and an eiderdown for covering. And on this deadly cold night Millican had, as is his wont, taken off his day clothes before he stretched himself out to sleep. Which of us accustomed to the luxury of a bed in a well warmed house would not have been frozen stiff? But Millican makes light of all severe kinds of weather.

And Millican glories in the life he leads. "I was a clerk in a London office. The life stifled me. I longed to be free. I gave up my job and ever since I have camped out. Today I live rent free, rate free, tax free. It's the only kind of life worth living." And a question about the 14 hours of black-out, without even the occasional glimmer of candlelight, he said, "Well, I don't sleep much, and while I am awake I lie and listen and think. There's a lot to think about just now, isn't there? All the sounds of the night, the roar of the mountain stream, the barking of cur dogs and foxes, the cries of birds, how can I be lonely with such company?" Millican told us a good deal about his philosophy of life, but that, of course, is not for public reading. Suffice it to say that the more you hear of his conclusions the greater your respect for the man.

Our curiosity about his domestic ways was, of course, keen. Soon we discovered that Millican is a vegetarian and believes that we can live on wholemeal bread. And, delving into one of his packing cases, he produced a bag of wholemeal flour and began to make it into dough, mixing with the flour the sultanas and currents soaking in water in tin canisters depending on an iron rod ingeniously suspended between the slates. The dough was a slab twice the size you could hold in your fist. Then, drawing together the birch logs smouldering on a rock, he fanned them with the lid of a flat canister. In a moment or two there was a bright fire, with the blue smoke curling up the rock face as though nature had designed a perfect way of getting rid of it.

It was still a mystery how the dough was to be baked. From another hole in the slates Millican pulled out a long-handled wire tray, such as housewives use for containing soap to be agitated in a dish washing bowl. Into the tray went the dough. The wire tray was fixed that it might be left and so in the course of a quarter of an hour we saw the bread start to bake. Very good bread it was, too. We tasted it afterwards and ate it, sultanas and raisins and all, with relish. "That's the foundation of my domestic economy." "And your principle meal?" "Oh, that's dinner in the evening. Wholemeal bread again, but, either I bake potatoes, or I boil them, together with carrots and other vegetables I may have been able to get. I am pretty expert at dinner meals. You see, when I camp in a tent and cook for a party that I have been taking in the hills, I have been in the habit of making four, five, or six courses. Simple dishes, if you like. Give me wholemeal bread, porridge, coffee and cigarettes and I am quite happy. I buy very good coffee at 2s 2d a pound. It's as nice as any coffee you may pay a lot more for."

You may have gathered now some insight into the life of Millican Dalton. Do not imagine, however, that he is a recluse. He goes down to the Post Office every day for his letters and a newspaper and he does his shopping in Keswick. Frequently he is visited by people who know him or of him. He is a busy man. He makes divers sorts of camp equipment. Tents are his speciality. Quite pardonably, he believes that a tent of his making takes a lot of beating. He is full of ideas about clothes. He claims to have been the inventor of shorts and his followers, he says, are to be numbered by the million including boy scouts. To sail to the sea from Borrowdale is one of his ambitions. We shall not be surprised if he designs a raft to take him to the Solway this summer. At the age of 73½ years he climbs as well as ever, though he says that he is more cautious than he used to be. When the days grow longer and warmer he will be called upon to act as a guide to visitors and he will conduct adventure parties, the adventures being entirely of his own creation. Even in wartime he will have plenty of scope for his energy among young outdoor folk.

Then, further fuelling the media frenzy, was a solo appearance in a *British Paramount* news feature after a camera crew had descended on the 'Cave Hotel.' The black and white clip, titled "Britain's Cavemen at Home," was released on 3rd March 1941 and shown at cinemas across the country.

Apparently the footage, part of the *Reuters TV* news archive, was never transferred from its original 35mm film to a modern format and, as with other parts of the archive, has tragically decomposed. Presumably, the footage may never be seen again. However, a catalogued script of the news feature still exists and reads:

The Lake District, Cumberland, England:

(LV*) Caveman leaving cave to collect firewood. (SV*) Cutting tree branches with saw. (LV) Carrying branches. (CU*) Walking towards camera with branches. (LV) Returning to cave with wood. View of living area. Caveman entering cave. (SV) Cooking a meal. (SV) Caveman sitting outside cave with meal – puts cigarette in-between his toes. (SV) Shot of cigarette in-between toes in preparation for eating his meal. (CU) Eating meal.

*[LV = Long View Shot, SV = Short View Shot, CU = Close-up shot].

Soon after Dalton's appearance in the *British Paramount* news clip he was confronted by P. H. D. and his wife in May 1941, they wrote:

"We spent a week at Grange-in-Borrowdale, memorable for our meeting with a quaint old character in shorts and a slouch hat we saw one day on Grange bridge looking over the upstream parapet. On impulse I went over to him and asked, "Excuse me, could you be Millican Dalton?" "Yes," he replied. "Do you perhaps remember my father H. G. D.?" "Of course, we climbed together. We carried our bikes over Sty Head – it would be about 1911." H. G. D. worked as a chemist in London, his brother-in-law, G. P. A. Richards, worked in insurance – hence the connection. "We had a long, quiet walk with him next day," continued J. H. D., "Up on the fells around Watendlath via Lodore Falls, accessing the falls along Dalton's own 'personal' path, to avoid the hotel charge of 2d, making tea besides the brook running out of the little lake. Tea making kit produced by Dalton, with a wood fire, of course. We returned to Grange via Rosthwaite. Dalton was very tired at the end. Later, a pencilled note from Dalton awaited us at the Post Office above Grange bridge and that evening we went to his cave. We found the cave in Castle Crag with some difficulty, rather a damp spot at the top of a great slate rubble heap. Millican Dalton has a semicircular wall of slate about 2 feet high adjoining one side, the space enclosed being perhaps 6' by 2'6". Here he has his fire, bed and seats and numerous little shelves for papers, books etc. All a bit dirty.

We sat down by the fire and he pulled a sort of sacking roof over our heads to keep out the draughts. The fire was soon kindled to a cheerful crackling glow and we sat talking for a good while. He talked of life and politics (he thought we were at war with the wrong enemy – it should be Russia not Germany). He is a great talker and though 74 does not repeat himself, though rather liable to be sidetracked. Dalton told us that he climbed Napes Needle solo, every spring, and if this ever became too much for him he would give up rock climbing. His old wrinkled face under the green velour hat looked magnificent in the firelight, with the paling sky behind him at the mouth of the cave. At nine-thirty we got up to go and Millican accompanied us down to the track running into Grange. It was almost dark and he turned back. It was just possible to find our way down to Grange in the velvet night when some few minutes later his fierce battle cry rang out from above us, echoing from side to side of the valley and J. H. D. answered with her own. Next day, Millican talked of health doctors and inoculation, he advised J. H. D. not to have our baby vaccinated. We avoided the subject of war, which had caused some heated discussion the night before. Millican always has some interesting topic ready to hand when necessary. He rode up to our lodgings on an incredibly old bicycle and we started along the Keswick road under his guidance for a round of Watendlath. After tea we visited Castle Crag but found Millican out. We broke up a pile of sticks for him and just as we were leaving we were hailed from below by the old man who had a good bundle of sticks on his shoulder. We said our goodbyes and after we had left gave him our call until the cliffs echoed but he cannot have heard for there was no reply."

Postal Address
P O Grange
Keswick

Aladdins Cave

Friday morning
2/5/41

Dear Friends

I'm off shopping to to Keswick - but shall be back home about 5.30 & shall be glad to see you later, when it suits you -

If you have an electric torch, you will be able to stay later at the cave - I have an acetylene bike lamp anyhow & can take you down as far as necessary - if it is dark -

I have of course coffee & tea here - but may have no milk - (I havent

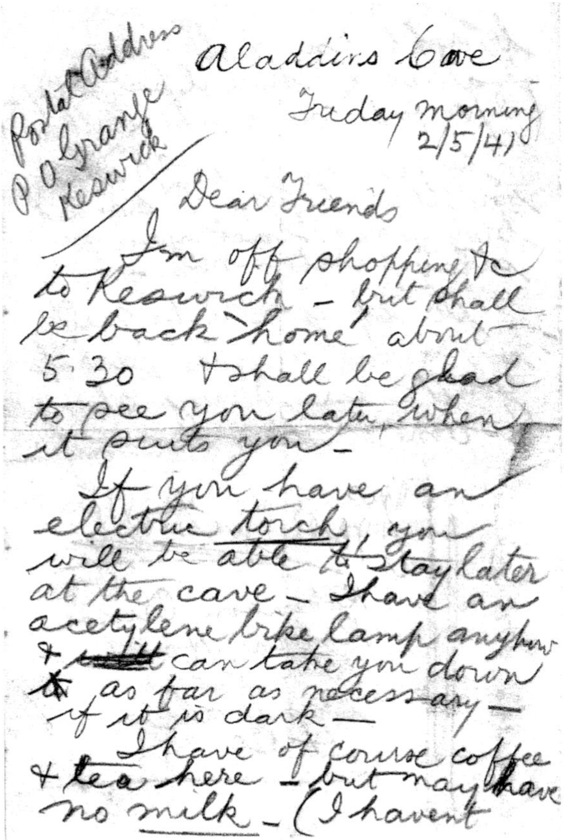

An invitation to tea. Dalton's pencilled letter to P.H.D. and wife.

bought any milk since I arrived here last July— (I prefer my drinks without) —Swiss milk is now rare in the shops— I too did buy some last year for stray visitors here—

So if you like milk in your drinks perhaps you can bring along some this evening—

Yrs Millican Dalton

Robinson Crusoe
Robin Hood
Rob Roy
Sinbad
& Co

Lieut Dale

Clearly a man of many names.

19
Farewell Millican Dalton.

M. D. next to the River Derwent c. 1940.

Towards the end of WWII Dalton considered his future as a guide and, after half century of guiding, eventually decided to retire – at around 75 years old! In the meantime Henry Dalton had died several years prior in May 1940 and was buried in the grounds of Jordans Meeting House. Millican, never one for mourning suits, attended the funeral dressed in his usual 'Robinson Crusoe' attire. Although now the only remaining child, he was seen by many folk all through his seventies, who commented on his lively and sprightly nature whether walking, cycling or climbing.

In 1945 he chose to spend Christmas with Henry's widow and children and to celebrate with traditional Christmas tree and yuletide trimmings. However, he was uncomfortable with the festivities and, regardless of much persuasion to stay, he left on Boxing Day and made his way up the Oxford road in the direction of Maidenhead.

Irrespective of retirement the Professor of Adventure continued with his annual summer visits to the Lake District, even as a late septuagenarian, with the 'Cave Hotel' remaining his chief residence.

It was from his cave in Castle Crag that Mabel M. Barker received an amusing letter posted without an envelope in 1946. It concerned a difference of opinion with Harold Spencer Jones, the Astronomer Royal: ("He said I was wrong, but I have reason to believe that he was") "I should have liked to have you dropping stones on them (his opinions on the universe!), and trying to dodge them." Millican, as energetic as ever, disclosed his immediate plans for the summers climbing. Commendably the veteran cragsman never regarded himself as past climbing even in his 80th year! Regardless of his hearty lifelong appetite for tobacco Dalton remained fit, strong and agile.

Summer in Borrowdale came to a close followed by the customary retreat south. On time the winter of 1946 arrived and, as usual, Dalton was still content camping out in his hut at High Heavens Camp. January 1947 proved to be worse than normal and witnessed the coldest weather of the century. Arctic conditions laid an icy hand over the entire country including Dalton's domain in which the nearby River Thames froze over. Many parts of the nation ground to a halt with schools and bus services being severely affected with problems exacerbated due to fuel shortages. With no respite, almost constant northerly winds kept average temperatures hovering around freezing point. Meanwhile, Millican, at an astonishing 79 years of age, was coping fine albeit aided by a well-stoked fire. However, one night, sometime at the beginning of January, the hut met the same disastrous fate as its Epping counterpart and was accidentally burnt down. With no specific explanation for the blaze it was assumed his cat had knocked over a candle (the fact that Dalton lit large fires in the hut would be a more probable reason for its ill-fate). Despite the dreadful weather he was adamant to remain at High Heavens Camp and immediately moved into one of his tents.

Unfortunately the winter conditions proved too much and he consequently became ill. After a number of weeks of illness he was admitted to Amersham Hospital where he remained an in-patient for several weeks, failing to respond to treatment. Millican Dalton died in hospital on the 5th February 1947 at the age of 79. As a result of the inclement weather he died of a combination of acute heart failure, pulmonary bronchitis and bronchopneumonia. Lying uncompleted by his bedside was Dalton's life work, *Philosophy of Life*, which had been started many years earlier. As would be expected for a man of his character he left no Will and Testament or Letters of Administration. The whereabouts of his lifework is uncertain – presumed lost.

In hindsight Millican Dalton must have found the freedom and romance he was searching for, as a return to conventional living was never made. Freedom was his life, which he found and announced, "Free I am as the buzzard mewing by day or the owl hooting by night. Freedom is everything." Summarizing his life, pictured in the press under the headline 'A Happy Lifer' a photograph showed Dalton sat on the step to his hut with the remarkable quote:

"After treating life as a chemical experiment I find that
the simplest life is the happiest."

An obituary appeared in the *Keswick Reminder* on Friday March 14th 1947. 'All those people who knew Millican Dalton, better known as the Borrowdale hermit, will learn with great sorrow of his passing last week. At the age of 79 years he died at Marlow, Buckinghamshire, in a hospital after weeks of illness. Millican Dalton turned his back on society and came to Borrowdale to lead the simple life. His home was a craggy cave on Castle Crag where he made his headquarters for his Spartan life on the fells he loved so well. Millican spent all his summers here where he was well known for the homely way he dressed and went about among folk of all grades and calibre. His tattered shorts, mountaineering sports coat and his Tyrolean hat complete with feather will always linger in the memory of those who knew him best. The world is much poorer for the loss of such men.'

After reading this article in the *Keswick Reminder*, his good friend Mabel M. Barker wrote an obituary for the F.& R.C.C. Journal 1947: 'His picturesque figure and loveable personality have surely become part of the heritage of Lakeland so long as the hills endure and men love them. It is difficult to strike a fair balance between his firm belief in his own opinions and his innate modesty; to assess his curious self-assertiveness, and the absence of any self-seeking. He had, I think, early worked out a theory of life for himself and if ever anyone did so, he lived up to it consistently and completely. He had found something, and was well content with it. Into this unison of theory and practice of life, climbing fitted as a natural part. He did things on the rocks, as everywhere else, to please himself, but not for self-seeking; to fit in with his theory of life and of earth and his relation to it. He believed that people (astronomers included) were "shutting their eyes to the foundations of the universe." Perhaps he was wiser than most of us, and his long and happy life indeed trod a pathway to the stars. I wonder how many owed to him their first thrills on rock and rope; in camp and caves in all weathers; in forest and on water, and in the cunning management of wood fires. Personally I owe him much.'

In the same Journal, Ralph H. Mayson added: 'He was a well known figure throughout Lakeland in his picturesque garb, respected by all who knew him. A man of simple pleasures and tastes, conductive to a mind at peace with the world, whose knowledge of things in general was very sound. After a day on the hills with him, or just pottering about, one had a feeling of contented happiness and peace of mind, proving the simple pleasures of life to be most lasting. He will be greatly missed as a companion and guide, made lasting by the Valley of Borrowdale and its hills, with Castle Crag, the guardian fortress of them all.'

R. E. Williams said, "His resources for adventure were never ending."

Many people became acquaintances with Dalton through contact with him in Borrowdale. One such person was A. Harry Griffin, climber and journalist, who said "He was just a 'character' – an unusual man who was only happy when he was in the hills, climbing, or in the woods and the rivers."

L. M. W. *Essex Review* 1948 – 'It is not all of us who can follow our dreams as wholeheartedly as Millican Dalton; indeed if any appreciable percentage of the community did so it would play havoc with the tidy plans of our administrators; but characters such as he are an admirable leaven and at his passing we can truly mourn the extinction of a 'candle which lights others while consuming itself.'

A tribute, overheard on the typically overcrowded Borrowdale bus not long after his death, was as follows: "Now a man like that has learned the great secret, the secret of going without so many things that we feel essential. He knows the comradeship of the fells and of all those who love them. He was a great gentleman and will be missed in the mountains."

20
Epilogue.

M. D. at the junction of Station Street and St John's Street, Keswick. (Carlisle Library)

For some reason the Professor of Adventure, his contribution to society and his association with the outdoor movement in particular, has been overlooked and masked by the passage of time and the promotion of other people and events. Millican Dalton is often mentioned, but never given the credit he justly deserves as one of Lakeland's, Essex's, Buckinghamshire's and British rock climbing histories greatest characters.

Although much information remains unearthed, with what facts are known he will be elevated from obscurity to his rightful position in England's heritage and the history books alongside the likes of Lakeland's Arthur Ransome and Essex's Sir Jacob Epstein. Unlike these characters, Dalton expressed himself in an understated way. Quitting work to pursue dreams, choosing home be it tent, hut or cave, his strange lifestyle and unorthodox, philosophical approach to life in general, distinguishes him as a true quintessential English character from his contemporaries in the 19th and 20th centuries.

Especially apparent was a complete lack of greed. Success in the commercial world would simply have been a matter of course and a more than comfortable lifestyle no doubt achievable. In preference to a life of comfort and ease was a life of simplicity. Dalton unequivocally possessed a genuine adoration of simple living, accepting that material items did not bring happiness or real satisfaction. His only want was romance and freedom – hardly a shameful ambition. Upon deserting work he woke each and every morning to a day that he could call his own. Each day was enjoyed hour by hour and the most was made of any situation. Happiness was achievable through freedom. Life in the outdoors was his symbol of freedom, made more significant with the associated proximity to nature and wildlife he so much adored. A lifetime's contentment in the open allowed for a union with nature, his companion with whom he never felt lonely. To enjoy nature to its full extent he chose to live amongst it, study it; watch its varying moods and changing features. He made friends with the rocks, peaks, lakes and rivers and they never proved false. It is almost certain something was found in the wilds as he upheld his alternative lifestyle for over half century without wearying.

Whatever his lifetime achievements, whether it be dismissing Victorian protocol with the groundbreaking guiding of mixed-sex groups or his experiments with lightweight gear, he is primarily revered for his aesthetic appearance and spirit of adventure which saw him roam the world for over 50 years searching relentlessly for thrills and danger.

It was this non-compliant, freethinking approach that reflected his laid-back, stress free outlook on life. Despite the laid-back approach and self-funding existence, he always maintained an action-packed life and a smart outward appearance irrespective of his homemade clothes. His homely appearance resulted in him commonly being perceived as a hermit, such as the Borrowdale Hermit. Although he did live something of a solitary existence, he was not a hermit in the true sense of the word. He was not a recluse and throughout life was socially active with friends, family and even strangers. Dalton was regarded as a true gentleman, universally liked by all who knew him because of his down-to-earth attitude and ability to accept and relate to all people regardless of their social status. It is possible that he was something of a self-publicist, but commendably, self-fulfilment was achievable without selfishness. Unlike some people who choose solitary existences, he had no argument with society and was far from anti-social. He chose to quit employment not to hide from society but to escape the rush and stress of conventional city life. In all fairness he dropped out decades before the phrase became fashionable and was, in a way, ahead of his time.

Considering his long, active and healthy life and, as importantly, his feisty appetite for tobacco, it seems highly unlikely that he suffered from rheumatism, consumption or neurosis – unless he knew more than the rest of society and the open-air life was indeed a cure!

Life, deemed as a suitable basis for a chemical experiment, was it seems worth gambling. To this basis he added a philosophy which, with the addition of simplicity and romance, made life much more fun. The discovery of this self-shaped, idealistic, dreamy world was the perfect answer to his quest and proved the theory behind his chemical experiment correct. His genius and courage to experiment with life must be applauded. This deep thinking philosopher was more than satisfied with his paramount enjoyment of life, well aware nothing was going to compromise it. Millican Dalton was totally dedicated. He made no show of it, simply did it, and then stayed with it. Such was his determination he refused to settle down and marry. Intimate relationships, yet to be disproved, are unlikely to have existed, but an open-minded view should be adopted. His charm, warm personality, his acceptance of women as equals and his localised fame would have definitely been an attraction, leaving the point open to speculation. Mabel M. Barker though not romantically linked with Dalton shared something with him – there was an obvious connection and a degree of chemistry between the two. Did their relationship ever go further? The fiery relationship enjoyed with Pixie Poole was also, supposedly, of an innocent nature. She chased him, having fallen in love, but he never entertained her. What was the full extent of their relationship? What was he doing in her caravan in the early hours of the morning? As a result of the dearth of relationships no children were born to carry on his legacy and provide an accurate insight into his way of thinking. Sadly, the exact basis of his philosophy may never be fully understood. If only a *Philosophy of Life* had survived, what enlightenment would be available to all? Without this explanation maybe some consideration should be given to whether lessons could be learnt from his search for romance and freedom and attention paid to the conclusion of his chemical experiment.

In the current age of social reform and political correctness Millican Dalton's life and achievements become increasingly mythical. Nonetheless a new generation of admirers, or modern day '*Daltonites*,' will ensure his name and symbol of freedom remains in England's heritage and his memory exists for years to come.

Millican Dalton
1867-1947
Professor of Adventure, Monarch of Borrowdale and Legendary Symbol of Freedom.

21
Acknowledgements.

Many thanks to all of the following who assisted with my research. Without their help this book would not have been possible.

Mum and Dad, family and friends who assisted in collating information.

Mr and Mrs L. Barker for their extremely warm welcome, trusting nature, photographs and help.

Librarians at Keswick, Billericay, Loughton and High Wycombe Libraries who helped even in my absence.

Staff and Archivists at Cumbria, Buckinghamshire and Essex County Records Offices.

The volunteers at Preston Temple of the Latter Day Saints Family History Centre who explained all.

Friends of the Society of Friends.

Members of Billericay Archaeological & Historical Society and Loughton & District Historical Society.

Dalton family members Nancy Sogge (nee Dalton) and Ann Yould (nee Dalton) who provided vital answers to questions.

Residents of Keswick, Marlow Bottom and High Wycombe for their anecdotes.

The Fell & Rock Climbing Club of the English Lake District for their photographs and articles.

The *Daily Mirror, Keswick Reminder* and the *Whitehaven News* for use of their articles.

Also many thanks to those not named who helped in one capacity or another with the compilation of this book. Finally I have made great efforts to locate the copyright owners of the Keswick Boot, if they exist, unfortunately without success. I have made use of this photograph and acknowledge that source with thanks.

Selective Index

Abraham, Ashley P. 39,42,43,61

Abraham Brothers 14,15,62,63

Abraham, George D. 39,40,43,61

Alston 4

Association of
Cycle Campers 9

Astronomer Royal 97

Austria 14,65

Baden-Powell, Robert 26

Band of Hope 5,33

Barker, Mabel M. 29,30,50,51-59,61,65,
67,70-73,81,86,97,99,
103

Beetham, Bentley 34,38,62,63

Billericay 13,42,47,48,104

Borrowdale 9,15,20,22,24,27,31,34,
35,41,42,44,50,52,56,
62-64,78,81-83,85,88-
94,98,99,103

Borrowdale Hermit 20,98,102

Borrowdale Yews 82

British Paramount 94

Brookfield School 4-6

Brownswood Road 6,7

Buzzard Chimney 35,62

Camping and
Caravanning Club 9

Castle Crag 56,79-83,94,95,97,99

'Cave Hotel' 78-80,82-84,86,90,94,
97

Chiltern Hills 74,75,77

Churchill, Winston 91

Cleopatra's Needle 64

Climbers Club 39,40

Cullin Hills 15,59

Daily Mirror 90,91,104

Dalton,
Elizabeth Crosby 4,6
Frances 4-6,53
Henry George 4,6-8,15,39,40,47,53,
74,76,77,97
John James 4
Joseph Crosby 4,6,7,47,53
William 4,6
William Tinniswood 4

Doves' Nest Crags 15,34-38,42,52,58,60,
62,64,82

Edmundson, Stan 83

Epping Forest 7,45,47,48,54

Eskdale 15

Esperenca 11

Essex 7,11,13,32,47,49,50,
101,104

Essex Review 9,99

Fell and Rock
Climbing Club 12,35,41-45,49,58,59,
61,62,81,83,88,89

Foulard 3,4

Gaspard, Josef 21

Geddes, Patrick 53,70,72

Glencoe 15

Grange-in-Borrowdale 32,41,79,81,82,87,94,
95

Haskett-Smith,
Walter Parry 9,42,45

High Beech 46

High Heavens Camp 74-76,98

High Lodore 20,22,50,56,63,78

Holding,
Thomas Hiram 8,9

Holiday Fellowship 21

Ireland 14

Isle of Skye 15,59

Jones, Harold Spencer 97

Jones, Owen Glynn 39,41,62

Kenmare Estuary 15

Keswick	14,22,28,32,33,45,54, 58,61-63,82,85,86,88-91,93,95,101,104
Keswick Reminder	98,99
Killarney	15
Lincoln Terrace	54
Loch Coruisk	15
Lodore Falls	15,22,94
London Lead Company	3,4,6
Loughton	49,54,75,104
Marlow Bottom	74,104
Matterhorn	15,40
Mayrhofen	67,72
Mayson, Ralph H.	14,15,33,44,58,61,80, 81,87,99
Millican, Tinniswood	4-6,54
Mumford, Lewis	72
Napes Needle	9,15,22,23,42,52,53,58, 64,89,92,94
National Trust	83
Nenthead	3-6
Pencoed Pillar	39,40,60
Pillar Rock	15,42-44,62,89
Plaskett, Ernie	32,52,82
Poole, Helen M. (Pixie)	75,76,103
Puttees	26,77,91,92
Quaker	3,4,54
Rannoch Moor	15
Robinson, J. W.	9,62
'Rogue Herries'	82,85-87
Scafell Pike	10,15,17,22,23,32,58, 64,81
Scotland	8,14,15,26
Seathwaite	42,50,51,58,81-83,92
Seathwaite Slabs	83
Sewing Machine	18,25,84
Shepherd's Crag	56,63
Shorts	25,26,52,83,91-94,99
Slingsby, Cecil	9,42,62,64,88
Snowdonia	38
Stanley Ghyll	15
Stony Path	54
Sty Head	8,58,81,94
Sunday Chronicle	3,62
Switzerland	14,15,21,67,72
Taylorgill Force	58,92
'The Camp'	13,47
Thornwood	11,13,48
Tirol	65,72
Wales	8,14,15,38,39
Walnut Cottage	54,74
Walpole, Hugh	45,85-87
Wasdale	10,17,18,21,41,60,62, 63
Wastwater Hotel	21,41
Whitehaven News	92,104
Wigton	4
Woodbine cigarettes	27,64,82